The Common and
Special Gifts of the
HOLY SPIRIT

The Common and Special Gifts of the
HOLY SPIRIT

A Deep Encounter with the Spirit of Jesus,
Who Was Sent to Us by Our Good Father God

JERRY MERCER

iUniverse LLC
Bloomington

THE COMMON AND SPECIAL GIFTS OF THE HOLY SPIRIT
A Deep Encounter with the Spirit of Jesus,
Who Was Sent to Us by Our Good Father God

iUniverse books may be ordered through booksellers or by contacting:

iUniverse
1663 Liberty Drive
Bloomington, IN 47403
www.iuniverse.com
1-800-Authors (1-800-288-4677)

ISBN: 978-1-4917-2376-0 (sc)
ISBN: 978-1-4917-2378-4 (hc)
ISBN: 978-1-4917-2377-7 (e)

Library of Congress Control Number: 2014901899

Printed in the United States of America.

iUniverse rev. date: 04/09/2014

This book was written to honor God, my wife, and my pastors, who by their tireless efforts have given me the faith and courage to delve into the mysteries of God and report on my findings.

My father in the faith has led my wife and me into greater faith, greater love, and a grand spiritual awareness.

God bless my wife, my pastors, and all who find the Master's way.

CONTENTS

Part 1: The Gifts of Revelation

Part 2: The Gifts of Power

Part 3: The Gifts of Encouragement

PREFACE

This book came into being by the Holy Spirit's leading and prompting, and its sole purpose is to advance the kingdom of God here on this planet, making the weak strong and the orphans to have a Father. Amen.

As an established theologian, I compiled thousands of hours into the teaching, researching, and revelation into the vastness of God, found in the Bible. God's Word was given to us, in the flesh, when He sent His Son, Jesus.

I am a responsible, faithful, and honest follower of the truth found in Jesus Christ and an ordained minister of the gospel.

As I wrote this book, I occasionally included clarifying information in parentheses to aid readers' comprehension of quoted text.

INTRODUCTION

This book was written to advance the kingdom of God and to make known all the great gifts God has bestowed upon us who believe. The gist of this book would be best suited to a maturing Christian, as it unlocks deep spiritual happenings and encounters that would require an ability to search out the findings in the scriptures and apply them to life situations.

CHRONOLOGY OF THE BOOK

The findings in this book follow a timeline dating back to 2005 and arriving into 2012. What started as a following of the Lord in 2005 has produced a deep encounter with the Holy Spirit of Jesus, culminating with happenings far beyond my own knowledge and expectations, into God's realm.

THE GIFTS OF REVELATION

CHAPTER 1

Common and Special Words of Wisdom
A natural and supernatural seeing into the
future, the things of God for us, His people

Part 1: Common Daily Wisdom:
"Remaining Reverent to the Word"

1 Corinthians 12:7 says, "Now to each one the manifestation of the Spirit is given for the common good."

We operate in common wisdom daily; God helps us in making practical decisions as simple as what to have for breakfast, how to plan our day, and how to follow Him fully. This common wisdom is for all who accept and seek after the things of God; He knows our hearts and responds to our faith. This faith in God allows His Holy Spirit to lead us by a Word or Words of Wisdom, used to fulfill a common task, with excellence!

In Job 28:12, Job asks a question: "But where can wisdom be found?" This question is answered in Job 28:28: "The fear of the

Lord—that is wisdom." Proverbs 4:7 states, "The beginning of wisdom is this: Get wisdom. Though it cost all you have get understanding." The Lord confides in those who fear Him; He makes His covenant known to them. A covenant is a mutual agreement between God and man, with conditions and consequences spelled out. Our covenant and promises from God are found in the Bible.

He gave us all power and authority in His Word, to use His Word, to seek His Word, and to fulfill His Word. He expects that of us. He gave us His only Son so that we could accomplish His Word; His Son left us a Helper, the Holy Spirit. Jesus said in John 14:16–17, "And I will ask the Father, and He will give you another advocate to help you and be with you forever—the Spirit of truth. The world cannot accept Him, because it neither sees Him nor knows Him. But you know Him, for He lives with you and will be in you. He, the Holy Spirit, is in us to help us walk out the daily plans and purposes of God."

We are given common words of wisdom to keep us reverent to the Master, allowing Him to guide our daily lives.

The words of wisdom might be defined as "a supernatural revelation of the mind and purpose of God communicated by the Holy Spirit." We must live aware; staying connected to the Word of God affords us a hearing and a completion of these common and special gifts of the Holy Spirit. Psalm 64:9 has the beginning of this common wisdom: "All people will fear; they will proclaim the works of God and ponder what He has done." Amen!

While reading the Bible one day and meditating about the spiritual gifts, I received a revelation to write a book. I had just purchased a book titled *Questions and Answers on Spiritual Gifts*, written by Howard Carter, and although I had never read it, I knew the gist of the book. My wife was downstairs reading the new book; when she came upstairs I told her of my revelation and all the parts of it. She excitedly said,

"That's exactly what that new book you bought is about." I knew the contents without ever reading the book. This revelation was a common gift of knowing as well as a common word of wisdom. I knew what to do now, and I knew of future events, although just enough for me to take the next step, not complete the book. I very quickly knew also that I needed to be prompt to do it, as God had spoken to my heart, "If you fail to do this, I will find someone who will." I knew this to be true from God's Word and Jesus' teaching about the talents found in Matthew 25:14–30.

The Bible tells us that Solomon had great wisdom, more than anyone before or after his time; Solomon shows us the benefits of wisdom in Proverbs 8:17–21 (Wisdom is speaking): "I love those who love me, and those who seek me find me. With me are riches and honor, enduring wealth and prosperity. My fruit is better than fine gold; what I yield surpasses choice silver. I walk in the way of righteousness, along the paths of justice, bestowing a rich inheritance on those who love me and making their treasuries full."

Paul prays for the Ephesians that God would give them the spirit of wisdom so they would know Him more. The spirit of wisdom is a defining characteristic of those who belong to the family of God. Jesus had this everyday wisdom from the Father once He realized who He was, and all He possessed in Him (Isaiah 11:2–3). It is common wisdom to follow the Lord's leading; He is in us and leads us by the Holy Spirit; that's why we covet earnestly these best gifts.

We also gain understanding as we operate in the will of God. God's will for us is taught, not given, as found in Psalm 143:10, which says, "Teach me to do Your will, for You are my God; may Your good Spirit lead me on level ground." What is God's will? It is His Word; it is how He created all things. God willed, and then He spoke; we too will then speak. Amen! Willing is a very strong power; it is the power of choice. As we are open to, and choose to, be led by the Holy Spirit, we purpose in ourselves to be blameless and faithful, thus ministering to God by our thoughts, our love for one another, and our actions. His common wisdom given to us is first of all pure, and then peace-loving, considerate, submissive, full of mercy and good fruit, impartial, and sincere (James 3:17). Wisdom sounds and reacts much like love; the wisdom of God comes from Love Himself. So get wisdom.

God commends and cares for us as we follow His way; we have an intuitive look at our now, as well as a seeing into our future. We must see (perceive) and do God's will for us; this affords us wisdom of the first degree. We must seek His way and never turn away from doing all the good we know to do—never complaining, never flattering for gain, never mocking, as these are symptoms of a hardening heart. A hardened heart leads us away from God—our only source of true wisdom! Jude has a great example in Jude 14–19. He discusses the ungodly folks, doing ungodly acts, living in ungodly ways; ungodly seems to be a common theme here. Jude goes on to explain about mockers who walk after their own ungodly lusts. These are sensual persons, who cause divisions, not having the Holy Spirit. We must refrain from flattery; flattery is a form of a lie, and we must never lie for any reason. A lie cuts us off from the power of God, making the gifts of the Spirit nonexistent in our lives.

We must have the Holy Spirit in manifestation to experience the gifts of the Spirit; let us covet earnestly these best gifts. We need the common and special gifts of the Spirit to sustain ourselves, the church, and those like believers we are commanded to love.

Psalm 111:10 sums up the common or daily words of wisdom: "The fear of the Lord is the beginning of wisdom." The rewards of wisdom come to all who obey Him; these rewards are found in Proverbs 3:16: "Long life in her right hand; in her left hand are riches and honor."

As God enriches our lives with the power of His Word, we grow closer to Him by our faith in His Word; this Word is where our wisdom is found. One word of wisdom can change our lives and all those around us forever; one word of wisdom will allow us to walk in the purposes of God for our life: "Get wisdom, get understanding; do not forget my words or turn away from them." This advice is found in Proverbs 4:5. In the book of Proverbs you will find thirty-one chapters of godly wisdom; the richness of these proverbs, when meditated upon, will give you this wonderful, powerful, common, or daily wisdom.

Let us covet earnestly these best gifts. Let us be doers of these words of wisdom; our Father is. He by wisdom created all things; we are given this wisdom by the Holy Spirit, and this is the year of the Holy Spirit. As we seek godly wisdom, we will receive all that God has planned for us. This receiving is found in 1 Peter 4:10: "Each of you should use whatever gift you have received to serve others, as faithful stewards of God's grace in its various forms." God gives us His wisdom in proportion to our reverence of Him; let us fear and be in awe of our God, who created all things. Wisdom was with God in the beginning (the Architect at His side); this same wisdom is given to us liberally, and we now know where this wisdom starts or is grasped from, *the fear of the Lord that is wisdom. Let us covet earnestly these best gifts.*

Part 2: Special Words of Wisdom, "To Give Future Guidance into a Situation, Person, or Place"

AS WE LOOK INTO THIS special word of wisdom, we will see a distinct contrast between the common and the special gifts of the Holy Spirit.

We receive and *teach* common gifts; we *receive* and minister the special gifts that are given as the Holy Spirit wills. First Corinthians 12:11 says, "All these are the work of one and the same Spirit, and He distributes them to each one, just as He determines"—each being one of two or more distinct individuals. This means we all have opportunity to receive this gift of special wisdom. We become distribution centers as we allow the Holy Spirit complete access into our lives, as we covet earnestly these gifts and seek to minister them to those He reveals to us by our inner witness. This inner witness is the prompting or unction of the Holy Spirit in us.

In the story of Jesus' presentation to God, Simeon had this prompting by the Holy Spirit in Luke 2:26–28: "It had been revealed to him by the Holy Spirit that he would not die until he had seen the Lord's Messiah. Moved by the Spirit, he went into the temple courts. When the parents brought in the child Jesus to do for Him what the custom of the Law required, Simeon took Him in His arms and praised God, saying …"

Simeon was in the right place at the right time because of his inner witness, because he was in tune with his spirit as well as the Holy Spirit. Amen!

The Holy Spirit is alive and well. He allows entry into the divine and special gifts of God's power, ministered through us the body, to those He wills. We should never refer to the Holy Spirit as "it"; the Holy Spirit is as real as we are. Remember, we are spirits, we live in a body, and we have a soul.

We learned in part 1 how the reverence of God allows us this first foremost gift, the word of wisdom. The word of wisdom can be defined as a supernatural revelation of the mind and purpose of God communicated by the Holy Spirit. He communicates with us through many channels—by an angel as with Gideon, in a vision as with Daniel, in dreams as with Joseph, by an audible voice as with Moses, and as an inner witness within us. He guides us toward the prize of the high call (a divine summons). So let us press on toward the goal to win the heavenly prize to which God in Christ Jesus is calling us upward.

A special gift of the word of wisdom was often given to Solomon, as we find in the book of 1 Kings. God gifted and graced Solomon in many areas, including insight and the understanding of principalities and powers, and gave him wisdom in the first degree. Solomon was wiser and greater than all who had lived to this point in time. This grace allowed him to create sayings and songs that numbered in the thousands. In 1 Kings 4:29–34 he describes plant life, animal life, birds, reptiles, and fish—astounding, one should presume. Kings and queens from around the world came to learn of and from his wisdom. Let us look back at the beginning of this passage. Where did Solomon's wisdom come from? God. God gave Solomon special words of wisdom and the insight into plant and animal life, public and political happenings, and brilliance in leadership, by special words of wisdom. Read the entire book of Proverbs, where Solomon by the inspiration of God gave us wisdom upon wisdom, insight upon insight, and on into the book of Ecclesiastes, where Solomon is believed to have shared his life's findings.

The resources within his experience were unequaled wisdom, vast wealth, pleasure in abundance, and extensive building projects. Special words of wisdom would still make one wise, very rich, full of joy, and an increaser of the kingdom of God. Amen!

"The Lord brought me (Wisdom) forth as the first of His works, before His deeds of old; I was formed long ages ago, at the very beginning, when the world came to be. When there were no watery depths, I (Wisdom) was given birth, when there were no springs overflowing with water; before the mountains were settled in place, before the hills, I (Wisdom) was given birth, before He (God) made the world or its fields or any dust of the earth. I was there when He set the heavens in place, when He marked out the horizon on the face of the deep, when He established the clouds above and fixed securely the fountains of the deep, when He gave the sea its boundary so the waters would not overstep His command, and when He marked out the foundations of the earth. Then I (Wisdom) was constantly at His side. I was filled with delight day after day, rejoicing always in His presence" (Proverbs 8: 22–30).

God saw and formed all creation; He spoke, and wisdom designed and built all things that are created. All creation is a direct revelation of the mind and purposes of God.

We, His people, are a special treasure; He set us apart from all other creation by breathing on and in us, His Holy Spirit! We are formed and fashioned by a design that cannot fail. He saw and created us before there was one; no devil in hell can overcome His design, and again we are fashioned by a design that cannot fail—the image of God Himself! This image was spoken over us by God in Genesis 1:26–27: "Then God said, 'Let Us make mankind in Our image, in Our likeness, so that they may rule over the fish in the sea and the birds in the sky, over the livestock and all the wild animals, and over all the creatures that move along the ground.'" We are in a God class. He created us that way; we as His creation and people have the use of His special word of wisdom, given as the Holy Spirit wills.

When we operate in the Wisdom of God, we can expect a long, full life, prosperity in all we do and in all we work for, and we will be honored for our service to God and to His people. God honors those who honor Him, as found in 1 Samuel 2:30: "For those who honor Me, I will honor, but those who despise Me, will be disdained."

God is faithful to every scripture He breathed; He will most certainly honor those who honor Him. When we honor His Word by keeping it, and doing it, He will honor us by performing His Word in our lives.

Jeremiah 1:12 tells us, "The Lord said to me, you have seen correctly, for I am watching to see that My word is fulfilled." That doing of the Word makes known to God that we are hearing Him. Throughout the entire Bible, God speaks a constant message to His people: "Keep hearing and hearing, do not harden your heart." We must be open to God's direction and realize that His Word contains much correction. This correction comes from many avenues; our openness to receive correction from the Word and godly counsel shows our growth in wisdom. Change should and must accompany our newfound wisdom; a doing of what we know shows God that we understand and that our faith is in Him.

So we first must become hearers, because faith comes by hearing the anointed Word. As we listen, the Word penetrates our natural sense of hearing and enters into our spirit, taking root in our hearts. The word *listen* actually means to hear something with thoughtful attention, giving consideration to the speaker. Listening is a form of humility (humility is not assertive, not showy, and does not feel superior). If you are always seeking to be heard, the opposite of humility is at work. The spirit of pride would be the opposite pull. Pride is never a receiver and, therefore, repels the common or special words of wisdom.

If we are going to boast, we should boast about Jesus, who has become for us wisdom from God—that is, our righteousness, holiness, and redemption. Therefore, as it is written: "Let him who boasts boast in the Lord." Amen! Knowing God is the greatest boast we can have. His wisdom is always pure; His power is absolute.

As we operate in the common gifts of the word of wisdom, and as we receive and minister the special gifts of the word of wisdom, let us remember to "covet earnestly these best gifts."

Yet!

CHAPTER 2

Common and Special Words of Knowledge
A natural and supernatural look at the direction
and counsel given by God for now use

Part 1: Common Knowing; from the Word We
Know Him More and More Intimately!

THE KNOWLEDGE OF GOD'S WORD is not the word of knowledge.

Knowledge of the scripture is obtained through studying the Bible; the word of knowledge comes by revelation, given to us by the Holy Spirit as He wills.

Looking back at our text, 1 Corinthians 12:7 says, "Now to each one the manifestation of the Spirit is given for the common good." Revelations are given to us by God to know and experience God's goodness more and more, and this knowing produces a sonship regarding God as our Father and acknowledging Jesus as our Brother; we have been called to be joint heirs, with Jesus, by God. In 1 Corinthians 1:9 we see this sonship: God is faithful, who has called you into fellowship with His Son, Jesus Christ our Lord. What an amazing calling, and by revelation into this scripture we receive a knowing of it, and this common knowing produces godlike responses and reactions.

By spending daily time in the Word of God, we are afforded insight into the mysteries of God's knowledge, which is stored up for us who believe. In Jeremiah 33:3, God says, "Call to Me, and I will answer you, and tell you great and unsearchable things you do not know." We will be shown the things of God that we do not know, shown into the plans and purposes of God, by the Spirit of God. One of the most amazing things to me about God is that He can make something known to you that you know nobody else knows, out of all that has been known. Astounding! We serve and reverence an awe-inspiring God.

By receiving common words of knowledge from God, Solomon summed up all his findings in Ecclesiastes 12:13: "Now all has been heard; here is the conclusion of the matter: Fear God and keep His commandment, for this is the duty of all mankind." Receiving common words of knowledge are at times life-changing. Think about how a word of knowledge changes sadness to happiness, as stated in the above scripture, making things harmonious that were causing you to be vexed or confused.

A great knowing came to Isaiah when he sent out a call to trust the Lord. "This is what the Lord says to me His strong hand upon me, warning me not to follow the way of this people: Do not call conspiracy everything this people calls a conspiracy; do not fear what they fear, and do not dread it. The Lord Almighty is the One you are to regard as Holy; He is the One you are to fear" (Isaiah 8:11–13). We were created to reference and honor our Creator; all our purpose is found in reverencing the Lord. When we stay in the Word, trust in the Word, and do the Word, our reverence of God grows stronger and stronger, and our faith abounds to every good work, and our trust exceeds our fears.

When our faith exceeds any natural weight, we are freed, loosed, set in motion toward a destiny of love and peace, found only in Jesus Christ.

A word of knowledge from the Master guides our daily lives; our pursuit of His words and their workings leads us out of death and destruction into harmonious joy with our Lord and Savior Jesus Christ. Do you know Him? Just as importantly, does He know you?

Second Timothy 2:20–26 covers changing into that faithful person: "In a large house there are articles not only of gold and silver, but also of wood and clay; some are for special purposes and some for common use. Those who cleanse themselves from the latter will be instruments for special purposes, made holy, useful to the Master and prepared to do any good work. Flee the evil desires of youth and pursue righteousness, faith, love and peace, along with those who call on the Lord out of a pure heart. Don't have anything to do with foolish and stupid arguments, because you know they produce quarrels. And the Lord's servant must not be quarrelsome but must be kind to everyone, able to teach, not resentful. Opponents must be gently instructed, in hope that God will grant them repentance leading them to knowledge of the truth, and that they will come to their senses and escape from the trap of the devil, who has taken them captive to do his will. So we must cleanse ourselves, making ourselves useful to the Master, led by the Spirit of God to do good."

All the works and revelations of God are spiritual—spiritual in origin and source, and spiritual in makeup and effect. We are spirits; we live in a body, and we have a soul. On one occasion God gave me this word of knowledge: "Spiritual people believe things others only dream of." On another occasion, when a loved one of mine was going through a time of wondering, after a CT scan, a doctor told her she had spots on her spine and uterus. One morning while I was reading the Bible, while meditating and pondering, God spoke to my heart, "You're faithful to My Word; I will be too." At this point my wondering stopped and my faith grew. I knew from reading His Word every day that He was always and all-together faithful to His Word. Amen! This was a common and special word of knowledge and wisdom, a knowing that now everything was handled and that everything to come was also taken care of—common in the sense that I was doing a natural thing, reading His Word, special because I knew that He had intervened in the situation and all was clear.

We proceeded to a nuclear testing of the entire body, and after the test was completed the doctor said "*all clear,*" a phrase I have since heard on more than one occasion, "All clear." What comforting words.

In Proverbs 19:23, we see this wisdom in the fear of the Lord, and it leads to life, the future of our existence; we see knowledge abiding in satisfaction, and by this wisdom and knowing, evil is not even capable of being near us. Amen! The scripture reads, "The fear of the Lord leads to life." Then one rests content, untouched by trouble; this trouble would be a vexing by evil, and no evil can touch a godly man or woman.

We are in control of our lives when we look to our Spiritual Guide, the Holy Spirit, who dwells in us and was given to us by God. Our own actions and thoughts accept His leading, or override it. We, by our yielding, make room for or shut out evil.

Romans 5:5 says, "And hope does not put us to shame, because God's love has been poured out into our hearts through the Holy Spirit, who has been given to us." He has been given to us, past tense, so we possess the same spirit and power that God made available to Jesus. We must walk in this common power daily, and as He sees opportunities He will use us to minister these special gifts by that power working in and through us. Amen! Let us covet earnestly these best gifts.

Yet!

Part 2: Special Knowing—Direction for the Now, Supernaturally Given!

A WORD OF KNOWLEDGE IS given for a specific situation, a particular person or place, handed down by God through His Holy Spirit, and is in us, used to benefit all surroundings, people, places, and things.

When we look at the raising of Lazarus from the dead, we see this spectacular word of knowing come forth in John 11: 4–44: "But when Jesus heard about it (Lazarus's great sickness) He said, 'Lazarus's sickness will not end in death. No, it is for the Glory of God. I, the Son of God, will receive glory from this.'" As the story proceeds, Jesus stayed in the place where he was for two more days (verse 6); down in verse 11 Jesus states, "Our friend Lazarus has fallen asleep, but I am going there to wake him up." The disciples said, "Lord if he sleeps he will get better," talking about a restful sleep. In verse 14 Jesus answers them plainly, "Lazarus is dead."

Further into this passage, Jesus tells Martha in verse 23, "Your brother will rise again." In verse 24, Martha said to Him, "I know he will rise again in the resurrection at the last day." Jesus said to her, "I AM the resurrection and the life. The one who believes in Me will live, even though they die; and whoever lives by believing in Me will never die. Do you believe this?" Martha acknowledges her belief in Him, and we see in verse 34, Jesus asks, "Where have you laid him?" As they arrived at the burial site, Jesus says to Martha, verse 39, "Take away the stone." Martha, the sister of him who was dead, said to Him, "Lord, by this time there is a bad odor, for he has been there four days." Jesus said to her, "Did I not tell you that if you believe you will see the glory of God?" Then they took away the stone from the place where the dead man was lying. Jesus lifted up His eyes and said, "Father, I thank You that You have heard Me. I knew that You always hear Me, but I said this for the benefit of the people standing here, that they may believe that you sent me." Now when He had said these things, He cried with a loud voice, "Lazarus, come out!" And he who had died came out bound hand and foot with grave clothes, and his face was wrapped with a cloth. Jesus said to them, "Take off the grave clothes, and let him go."

We see the special word of knowledge that Jesus received in verse 4, spoken in verse 44, and working in and for Lazarus, and the people around the grave site. This Word produced belief in what they already knew, a higher understanding of the resurrection of the dead, Jesus, as He is in all things, and used this as a glimpse of His and our resurrection power. Amen!

What a glorious showing of a special word of knowledge and how it was used in the now, and also forever true. That truth being, "I am the resurrection and the life"—do you have, and have experience in this eternal life?

Another example of the special word of knowledge is found in John 8:4–11: "Teacher, this woman was caught in the act of adultery. In the Law Moses commanded us to stone such women. Now what do You say?" They were trying to get something on Jesus, trying to separate Him from the Law of Moses, but He bent down and started writing on the ground, pondering possibly, waiting most assuredly, for a special word of knowing, a word from God to reproof a group of fault finders, and a comforting word for a sinning woman. In verse 7 Jesus responds to the questioning, "Let any one of you who is without sin be the first to throw a stone at her." Again He stooped down and wrote on the ground. At this, those who heard began to go away one at a time, the older ones first, until only Jesus was left, with the woman still standing there. When Jesus straightened Himself up, He said to her, "'Woman, where are they? Has no one condemned you?' 'No one, sir' she said. 'Then neither do I condemn you,'" Jesus declared. "Go now and leave your life of sin." Jesus uses compassion to show Himself true;

He uses special words of knowledge to defuse a situation and to grant repentance to a sinning woman.

God is no respecter of persons; He will use us, His people, to do the works of Jesus, and our hearing from God is produced by our passion for the things of God. The more we know the Word, the more we know God; God gave us the Word in the flesh, by giving us Jesus.

In Luke 1 we see this Holy Spirit–conceived child of the Most High God! In Luke 1:28, we see the angel of the Lord coming to Mary with a greeting from God; what a word of knowing was presented to Mary this day, a word so powerful it troubled her at first. In verse 30, we see the angel's response to her: "'Do not be afraid, Mary, you have found favor with God. You will conceive and give birth to a son, and you are to call him Jesus. He will be great and will be called the Son of the Most High. The Lord God will give Him the throne of His father David, and he will reign over Jacob's descendants forever; His kingdom will never end.' 'How will this be,' Mary asked the angel, 'since I am a virgin.' The angel answered, 'The Holy Spirit will come upon you, and the power of the Most High will overshadow you. So the holy One to be born will be called the Son of God. Even Elizabeth your relative is going to have a child in her old age, and she who was said to be unable to conceive is in her sixth month.' For no word from God will ever fail. 'I am the Lord's servant,' Mary answered. 'May your word to me be fulfilled?' Then the angel left her."

May it be unto me, as You, God, have said. God has a word for all of our lives. He prophesized over each one of us; our quest is to find out what God says to and about us, and do it! This puts our faith in His Word, and makes our lives full and fulfilled!

Mary also had a special word of knowledge in John 2:5: "Do whatever He tells you." This command enabled Jesus to perform His first of many miracles: "Whatever He says to you, do it." When God speaks to our hearts, we must receive the Word, and do it; our trust is in Him; as we are in-filled and led by the Holy Spirit, we become more and more confident in His leading. We become great listeners, and great doers of God's desire for our lives, and His desire is always good.

Colossians 2:3–5 says it best: "In Whom are hidden all the treasures of wisdom and knowledge. I tell you this so that no one may deceive you by fine-sounding arguments. For though I am absent from you in body, I am present with you in spirit and delight to see how disciplined you are and how firm your faith in Christ is."

We stand unified in the faith, faithful to Him and to one another, full of power, full of wisdom, and basking in His goodness. Amen! What a great place to abide, a joint heir with Jesus: "The Son is the radiance of God's glory and the exact representation of His being, sustaining all things by His powerful Word" (Hebrews 1:3).

His Special Word of Knowledge to us: let us covet earnestly these best gifts.

Yet!

CHAPTER 3

Common and Special Discerning of Spirits
Our natural and supernatural abilities to
perceive and see into the spiritual realm

Part 1: Common Gifts in the Discerning of the Spiritual; Common Discernment Is Our Daily Discerning between Flesh and Spirit!

THE COMMON DISCERNMENT OF MAN comes from the common wisdom of man, and leads to the special gifts of the word of knowledge and to the discerning of spirits.

Proverbs 8:12–18 says, "I, Wisdom, dwell together with prudence; I possess knowledge and discretion. The fear the Lord is to hate evil; I hate pride and arrogance, evil behavior, and perverse speech. Counsel and sound judgment are mine; I have insight, I have power. By me kings reign and rulers issue decrees that are just; by me princes govern, and nobles— all who rule on earth. I love those who love me, and those who seek me find me. With me are riches and honor, enduring wealth and prosperity."

All this by discerning into the spiritual, acquired by being Holy Spirit led, led into a distinguishing between flesh leading to death, and the Spirit leading to life and fulfillment. Amen! This discerning of spirits allows us a knowing of all spirits, good or bad. The ability to see the presence, or activity, of a spirit being comes only through a revelation, which God gives by the Holy Spirit.

God gives this gift, and it is unaided by the natural mind. The Bible talks about mind renewal in Romans 12:2: "Do not conform to the pattern of this world, but be transformed by the renewing of your mind. Then we will be able to test and approve what God's will is—His good, pleasing and perfect will." The definition of renew is to make new spiritually, or as we read in 1 Corinthians 2:16, "For who knows the mind of the Lord so as to instruct Him? But we have the mind of Christ." We have the mind of Christ; we can be led by the Holy Spirit of Christ. He left us His Holy Spirit that we could imitate the things of God.

We also need mind *removal* to perceive the spiritual; as we look to the spiritual, we need the abilities of the spiritual; praying in tongues for self-edification allows this removal of our natural mind and gets us in tune with our spirit. By removal (the getting rid of whatever is useless), we align ourselves with the Spirit of God, ridding ourselves of the flesh that slows us down, or hinders our spiritual progress. So it takes a spiritually fit mind to see into the Spirit, to discern the Gifts of the Holy Spirit.

God gives us His Word on this glorious life in the Spirit in 1 Corinthians 2:9–10: "However, as it is written: 'What no eye has seen, what no ear has heard, and what no human mind has conceived' the things God has prepared for those who love Him—these are the things God has revealed to us by His Spirit. The Spirit searches all things, even the deep things of God." Do you love God? It takes the God kind of love to experience the Spirit of God, for God is love. This love is a spiritual condition, not a feeling.

In John 3, John's disciples are questioning as to why Jesus is baptizing more people than he was. John from his birth had a discerning into the spiritual; he was appointed to it by God even before his birth. In John 3:27–28, John answers his disciples, "A person can receive only what is given them from heaven. You yourselves can testify that I said I am not the Messiah but am sent ahead of Him." John discerned into the spiritual daily; he was never confused as to what God's plan for his life was—he was the voice crying out, "Prepare the way of the Lord." A gift from heaven as stated above, we all have a powerful gift, a witnessing gift, and a touching gift that is ours personally, assigned from God, from the heavenly realm. This heavenly realm is touched and perceived in and by the Holy Spirit in us, the common gift of the discerning of the spiritual, a living testament of God's will for us who believe. Seeing into the spiritual is an everyday practice; in Job 19:25–27, Job had this seeing when he stated, "I know that my Redeemer lives, and that in the end He will stand on the earth. And after my skin has been destroyed, yet in my flesh I will see God; I myself will see Him with my own eyes—I, and not another. How my heart yearns within me." *Seeing* God—our inner perceiving goes into the next life with us.

We should spend all of our lives building a mental picture of heaven; as we visualize heaven and see ourselves there, we are operating in godly-by-faith seeing, and this seeing will afford us entry, through Jesus. Commonly seeing into the spiritual realm is defined by the word *see*, which means to: (a) form a mental picture of, or (b) to apprehend by sight. *Apprehend* is to lay hold of, so we must stay focused on the Word and spiritual things—truth, honesty, integrity—and keep our inner seeing fastened to God and His provision, thus laying hold of the spiritual things of God.

As we live life by the Spirit of God, we see sin eliminated—this elimination of sin, this shedding of the weights that hold us back from all God has to offer. This conflict warring in us is resolved, and victory is ours, through Jesus Christ our Lord. Paul tells us about this in Galatians 5:18–23: "But if you are led by the Spirit, you are not under the law. The acts of the flesh are obvious: sexual immorality, impurity and debauchery; idolatry and witchcraft; hatred, discord, jealousy, fits of rage, selfish ambition, dissensions, factions and envy; drunkenness, orgies, and the like. I warn you, as I did before, that those who live like this will not inherit the kingdom of God. But the fruit of the Spirit is love, joy, peace, forbearance, kindness, goodness, faithfulness, gentleness, and self-control. Against such things there is no law." Verses 19–21 show us a life and character that lead to destruction and death, oblivious to the Holy Spirit but yielding to evil spirits. Verses 22 and 23 show us what the lives of spiritual people look like, full of good spirits and always doing good to and for all.

We truly are led and controlled by spirits; what we yield ourselves to, we become like. Whatever spirit or spirits we yield to, we take on that spirit's characteristics, so taking on a lying spirit would make you a liar; taking on a greedy spirit would make you a taker, and so on.

As we stay in God's Word daily, we take on godly characteristics; as we act on His Word, we become more and more like the Master. We must stay in tune with the Holy Spirit in us, as we read in Galatians 5:25, "stay in step with the Spirit of God." He is real, and He is real *good*. He produces life.

I like to say it this way: "Bible opened, not deceived; Bible closed, deceived."

We have a part in nourishing God's Holy Spirit in us, given to every believer that will receive Him. As we study the written Word, all those evil spirits start falling off; we become lighter and lighter, thus allowing us to rise, yes, resurrection power! We have this power through Jesus Christ our Lord and Savior. One of my favorite scriptures is found in Matthew 28:6: "He is not here; He has risen, just as He said." A common discerning into the spiritual affords us this knowing, a knowing that Jesus rose from the dead, and so will we.

This is part of our daily living, our daily confessing; we should always see Jesus and ourselves as *"Risen."* Romans 14:9 says, "For this very reason, Christ died and returned to life so that He might be Lord of both the dead and the living." We serve the God of the living as well as the God of those who have gone on before us. Amen! God is always a prayer away; we have a common discerning of the Spirit every day we look to God to meet our needs.

He is worthy of our asking.

David in the Psalms asked and kept on asking, and he received. Psalm 86:7 says, "When I am in distress, I call to You, because You answer me." David also would tell God how much he honored Him in Psalm 89:8: "Who is like You, Lord God Almighty? You, Lord, are mighty, and Your faithfulness surrounds You." David always knew that he could ask of God and that God was faithful to respond. If we are faithful to God's Word, He will be too! The faithful are those who practice faith; faith is a heartfelt belief but also requires a subsequent action.

Faith is produced from our working in and through the Word of God; faith allows the spiritual to become reality, which is actually part of the definition of *manifest*, which is how God and His Holy Spirit are discerned by us. This faith is in God and His abilities to do His Word in our lives, not a production by us; God is our Choreographer and our Producer.

Wisdom (which is the reverence and honor of God) is the beginning of all our faith, discernment, and trust in God, and is found in Proverbs 8:32–35: "Now then, my children listen to me; blessed are those who keep my ways. Listen to my instruction and be wise; do not disregard it. Blessed are those who listen to me, watching daily at my doors, waiting at my doorway. For those who find me (Wisdom) find life and receive favor from the Lord." Wisdom is a spiritually discerned quality that controls and makes wise all those who follow God's principles. Wisdom cannot be gathered by books or teachings, or by any other natural means. God-type wisdom is absorbed and gathered by our honoring God.

Our common but supernatural discerning of spirits comes from our intimacy and reverence to God. The Bible definition of Wisdom is: the ability to discern between right and wrong. Colossians 2:2–3 portrays love as a bond to wisdom: "My goal is that they will be encouraged in heart and united in love, so that they may have the full riches of complete understanding, in order that they may know the mystery of God, namely, Christ, in whom are hidden all the treasures of wisdom and knowledge." The things of God are considered treasures— priceless qualities that we lay hold of by our faith and pursuing of Him and His ways. Amen! These treasures are to be acquired by a constant and eager seeking of God and His plans for our lives. He has for us wisdom, a godly knowing of His secret plan for our lives and for His entire creation.

True wisdom is the art of living as God planned! All His creation is waiting to see the sons of man revealed. Let us covet earnestly these best gifts of the Holy Spirit!

Yet!

Part 2: The Special Gift of Discerning of Spirits, or Spiritual Special Discerning Is a Gift to Distinguish into the Spirit of Good and Evil, and to Proclaim Direction

IN THE FIRST CHAPTER OF the book of John, John talks about the coming of the Messiah; it was his calling in life to be the forerunner of Jesus. He was very confident in who he was, and in who Jesus was. We have this same confidence in God, who called us to be in companionship and participation with His Son Jesus Christ. In 1 Corinthians 1:9 we find this fellowship: "God is faithful, who has called you into fellowship with His Son, Jesus Christ our Lord."

In John 1:32 we see John giving further evidence of Jesus' lordship. "John gave further evidence, saying, 'I saw the Spirit come down from heaven as a dove and remain on Him.'" Jesus was and is engulfed by the Holy Spirit. His teaching came from Him; His healings came from Him; His life, death, and resurrection came from Him. Amen! John was born and lived to discern into the spirit; he had this special gift given to him on many occasions, although the gift was not his to possess. By following God's plan for our lives, we should be operating in these same gifts that the Holy Spirit directs into this world today. Our evidence of these gifts is found in 1 Corinthians 12:11: "All these (gifts, achievements) are the work of one and the same Spirit, and He distributes them to each one, just as he determines." By acknowledging the Holy Spirit, by coveting earnestly the best gifts of the Holy Spirit, we *all* should be operating in one or more of these gifts. These gifts knit us together and cause brotherly concern and compassion for like believers, and are actually the one command that Jesus gave us on many occasions: "Love one another." Love allows us a maturity into the things of God and affords us a sharing of, and participation with, the gifts of the Holy Spirit, namely in this chapter, the special discerning into the spiritual.

Let us look in 1 Kings to see a special discerning into the spirit, given at a supernatural level, to King Solomon. First Kings 3:7–14 says, "Now, Lord my God, You have made Your servant king in place of my father David. But I am only a little child and do not know how to carry out my duties. Your servant is here among the people You have chosen, a great people, too numerous to count or number. So give Your servant a discerning heart to govern Your people and to distinguish between right and wrong. For who is able to govern this great people of Yours?"

It pleased the Lord that Solomon had asked this, and God said to him, "Since you have asked for this and not for long life or wealth for yourself, nor have asked for the death of your enemies but for discernment in administering justice, I will do what you have asked. I will give you a wise and discerning heart, so that there will never have been anyone like you, nor will there ever be. Moreover, I will give you what you have not asked for—both wealth and honor—so that in your lifetime you will have no equal among kings. And if you walk in obedience to Me and keep My decrees and commands as David your father did, I will give you a long life." Long life in one hand, riches and honor in the other; that's what the Wisdom of God provides us. Proverbs 3:16 says, "Long life is in her (Wisdom's) right hand; in her (Wisdom's) left hand are riches and honor." We see this provision from God for all of us who seek Him diligently. In the passage in Kings, we see Solomon actually humble himself before God, knowing that in and of himself, he could not receive the charge of leading such a great people, God's people. Solomon asked of God for direction and ability, not material provisions, and God blessed Solomon because of his trust in God and afforded him the spiritual wherewithal to lead a vast number of people. He used his God-given, special discerning between good and bad to lead the people, to govern the people, and to judge the various complaints and lawlessness of the people.

It takes a close following of God to walk in the virtues of God; we can follow Him fully by staying in the Word of God daily. We have so much given to us, so many examples and teachings from His Word to tackle any natural or spiritual happenings. We must be open and able to hear from God and to receive the things of God.

Listening is the art of hearing, but we must go deeper than the ear canals on the side of our heads. We must hear and see internally, by the Spirit, the Holy Spirit in us. Amen!

Solomon had this ability to hear and discern, sometimes instantaneously, and at the time of a critical judgment. In 1 Kings 3:16–28, we see two prostitutes who came to the king and stood before him. One of them said, "Pardon me, my lord. This woman and I live in the same house, and I had a baby while she was there with me. The third day after my child was born, this woman also had a baby. We were alone; there was no one in the house but the two of us. During the night this woman's son died because she lay on him. So she got up in the middle of the night and took my son from my side while I, your servant, was asleep. She put him by her breast and put her dead son by my breast. The next morning, I got up to nurse my son—and he was dead! But when I looked at him closely in the morning light, I saw that it wasn't the son I had borne." The other woman said, "No, the living one is my son; the dead one is yours." What a great judgment Solomon has to make. At that very moment God gave him a special discerning into the spiritual, and he gave a charge; as we see in verse 24, Solomon said, "Bring me a sword." So they brought a sword for the king. He then ordered, "Cut the living child in two and give half to one and half to the other." The woman whose son it was would rather her son live with the lying woman than die, so she speaks out of compassion, "Please, my lord, give her the living baby! Don't kill him!" The lying woman said, "Neither I nor you shall have him. Cut him in two!" Then the king gave his ruling: "Give the living baby to the first woman. Do not kill him; she is his mother." What a great discerning of the spiritual; there was a lot going on in this story besides Solomon's great administration of justice. When we try to attain what others have, at their loss, we are partnering with the devil; he steals, kills, and destroys. Whatever spirit we partner with, we take on that spirit's characteristics. The evil lady in the story partnered with a lying and stealing spirit. The common and special discerning of spirits will always shine light on deception and cause right judgment to prevail; Solomon had this discerning, and it was associated with wisdom. Amen!

We are spirits; we live in a body, and we have a soul.

As spiritual people, we have the power that the Holy Spirit provides us; we can be led by Him, governed by Him, and make right decisions through Him. It is our inner man that, commonly and specially, discerns into the spiritual.

In Acts 6:5, we see Stephen, a man full of faith and of the Holy Spirit. Verse 8 has more description of Stephen, a man full of God's grace and power; this combination of faith, Holy Spirit, grace, and power allowed Stephen to perform many miracles and signs among the people. Religious people took offense at Stephen's power and found men to lie about him so they could pronounce a death sentence upon him, because they could not contend with Stephen's wisdom and the Holy Spirit's power in him. The religious leaders did find fault with Stephen, and he was stoned. But as Stephen neared death, he did not experience death. What he experienced was a spectacular seeing into the spiritual as found in Acts 7:55–56: "But Stephen, full of the Holy Spirit, looked up to heaven and saw the glory of God, and Jesus standing at the right hand of God. 'Look,' he said, 'I see heaven open and the Son of Man standing at the right hand of God.'"

What a special discerning into the spiritual; Stephen distinguished spiritual life instead of natural death. That, my friend, is what we all are created to do. Amen!

Let us covet earnestly these best gifts.

Yet!

THE GIFTS OF POWER

CHAPTER 4

*Common and Special Gifts of Faith
A natural and supernatural power, given by God,
to bring the nonexistent into existence*

Part 1: The Common Gifts of Faith, Which
Are Our Trust and Belief in God That Comes
by Hearing the Anointed Word of God

"Now FAITH IS CONFIDENCE IN what we hope for and assurance about what we do not see" (Hebrews 11:1).

Confidence comes from the word *confide: to show confidence (trust) by imparting secrets.* God shows His faith in us by revealing His secrets and mysteries to us; these revelations must be acknowledged and accepted by us through faith. Faith is, and has, substance; faith is not baseless. We base our faith on what God says in His Word, by an anointed Word from our preachers, and by the Holy Spirit's leading.

Faith operates when we do the Word; our trust in God and His Word allows us to do what we have received, thus becoming a doer of the Word. Faith without doing is likened to deceiving yourself, as we find in James 1:22: "Do not merely listen to the Word, and so deceive yourselves. Do what it says." Verse 23 goes on to say that if we don't become activators of the Word, we forget what we have received and lose the liberty the Word has produced in us, but if we do the Word we will be blessed in our doing. In Romans 4:17 we see this godlike faith: "God, who gives life to the dead and calls into being things that were not." How would things that didn't exist know what they looked like? He saw them by faith; that same faith caused their creation. The nonexistent must have faith to hook up with, to come into existence. Amen!

Let us look at some examples of common or daily faith. In Romans 10:17, we see the base scripture of how faith comes. "Consequently, faith comes from hearing the message, and the message is heard through the word about Christ." When faith is quickened in our hearts, and we believe that Jesus is our Lord and Savior, we speak out, and this speaking out of our heart is how we are saved. We acquire and use this same action in all other areas of faith—for protection, healing, power to do, and salvation.

Romans 14:23 states, "And everything that does not come from faith is sin." Faith originates in and comes out of our heart, our inner man, our spirit, and the opposing factor to our walking by faith, and that which leads to sin, is our flesh or natural man. This warring flesh could be defined as human nature without God. Galatians 5:17 explains further, "For the flesh desires what is contrary to the Spirit, and the Spirit what is contrary to the flesh." They are in conflict with each other, so that you are not to do whatever you want. These two powers are antagonistic to each other, a continual conflict. True faith does not consider any outside opposition; true faith justifies and accepts as righteous those inner leadings, and rules out pride, boasting, and self-righteousness. Knowing that God is the base of our faith, and hearing His Word and receiving His Word is where our faith originates.

So common faith comes by hearing the anointed Word of God, and this anointing works by God's Word having unity with our hearts. Amen! God spoke this phrase to me (not in an audible voice but inside), "The anointing is God placing His power on His word, in your life." This power is quickened and increases as our faith increases—faith working through love. True faith removes obstacles, faith that lifts weights of oppression, and faith that leads to righteousness (right standing with God), and this true faith pleases God. Hebrews 11:6 says, "And without faith it is impossible to please God, because anyone who comes to Him must believe that He exists and that He rewards those who earnestly seek Him."

God rewards faith—faith in all He has done and is still doing for us, His people.

God will always respond to faith; faith comes up in us by the Holy Spirit delivering to us promptings, inner leadings from God, that when acted upon produce faith responses, subsequent actions based on our receiving from Him. It pleases God when we step out on what we have received. He then has a place in our lives to produce great things, great prosperity, great healings, and great ministering of His common and special gifts of the Holy Spirit.

Let us remember to covet earnestly these best gifts.

In Mark 5:27–34, we see this faith, which produces *power*: "When she (the woman with an issue of blood) heard (how does faith come?) about Jesus, she came up behind Him in the crowd and touched His cloak, because she thought, 'If I just touch His clothes, I will be healed.' Immediately her bleeding stopped and she felt in her body that she was freed from her suffering." The key to this great passage is that she heard, and then acted on what she heard; this action produced her feeling. Feeling comes after faith; faith is not a feeling. Faith (the power) in her heart produced her actions, resulting in a feeling, and not only a feeling, but a healing, an instant cure. What part of her do you think heard? We know that faith comes by hearing, and hearing by the anointed Word of God; this hearing came into her spirit, and then her spirit overrode her flesh, resulting in faith to be healed, pulled from Jesus, as we see by going further in this passage.

We truly are spirits; we live in a body, and we have a soul! Our God-created spirit, who we really are, hears the Word of God; our spirit then has dominion over our flesh (human nature without God), resulting in godlike foreordained results, *by faith*.

This faith is our trust in God to perform His Word in our lives; we are hearers and doers, just as the woman with the issue of blood.

We see another faith by hearing in Luke 5:18–20, "Some men came carrying a paralyzed man on a mat and tried to take him into the house to lay him before Jesus. When they could not find a way to do this because of the crowd, they went up on the roof and lowered him on his mat through the tiles into the middle of the crowd, right in front of Jesus." When Jesus saw their faith, He said, "Friend, your sins are forgiven." If we look back in verse 17, we see that the power of faith was with Jesus to heal. Jesus responded to a joint faith; the man had faith, but his friends were also in faith. We need faith buddies; we need help at times; we need encouragement at times; we need *no quit* bulldog faith at times.

Both this man and the woman with the issue of blood had to push through crowds, overcome obstacles, keep on in the Word they heard, and then receive the end of their faith. Faith has a beginning (hearing) and an ending (doing), and always produces overcoming results based on God's ability to perform His Word in our lives. Amen!

We see in Luke 6:17–19 that faith coming again by hearing. "He (Jesus) went down with them and stood on a level place. A large crowd of His disciples was there and a great number of people from all over Judea, from Jerusalem, and from the coastal region around Tyre and Sidon, who had come to hear Him and to be healed of their diseases. Those troubled by impure spirits were cured, and the people all tried to touch Him because power was coming from Him and healing them all." They came to listen and be cured, they came to touch and feel the power present in Him to heal them. They must have heard of this power prior to making the trip—heard of Jesus and His good deeds.

We see yet another example of the gift of common faith in Acts 14:8–10, when Paul is speaking, proclaiming the good news: "In Lystra there sat a man who was lame. He had been that way from birth and had never walked. He listened to Paul as he was speaking. Paul looked directly at him, saw that he had faith to be healed and called out, 'Stand up on your feet!' At that, the man jumped up and began to walk." The crippled man, who had never walked, heard Paul preaching the good news, and the man's faith (inner spiritual self) received his healing, and in this passage he also received a miracle because he had never walked or learned how to walk; he went from crippled to leaping and walking. Miraculous!

Paul was a vessel, being used by the Master, an extension of His power transferred to the earth. Is what you are hearing allowing you this transfer of power?

The Word and its presentation by an anointed proclaimer will cause this power to work through us, God's people.

Let us ponder on what we are hearing. Is it motivating us to seek Jesus? Is our spirit being quickened and encouraged? Is our flesh prevailing in hearing too much worldly news, too much secular music, too much gossip? We need to take heed to what we are hearing. Psalm 119:9 says, "How can a young person stay on the path of purity? By living according to Your word." We must hear the Word of God continually to stay in the faith, faith that produces salvation, healing, freedom, and prosperity.

A great church and pastor are the best ways to hear and heed the anointed Word of God; be led by your spirit to the right church family. Do not settle.

Paul, the apostle, talks about this in Titus 1:1–3: "Paul a servant of God and an apostle of Jesus Christ to further the faith of God's elect and their knowledge of the truth that leads to godliness—in hope of eternal life, which God, who does not lie, promised before the beginning of time, and which now at His appointed season He has brought to light through the preaching entrusted to me by the command of God our Savior." Faith and truth are key elements in this church family; faithful believers do not lie. God has never lied and never will. We must emulate this character to remain in the faith. Our faith is our trust in God, who cannot lie; we as faithful ministers and people cannot lie either.

In Titus 2 we get some light on teaching: "You however, must teach what is appropriate to sound doctrine. Teach the older men to be temperate, worthy of respect, self-controlled, and sound in faith, in love and in endurance. Likewise, teach the older women to be reverent in the way they live, not to be slanderers or addicted to much wine, but to teach what is good. Then they can urge the younger women to love their husbands and children, to be self-controlled and pure, to be busy at home, to be kind, and to be subject to their husbands, so that no one will malign the word of God."

True faith and true teaching is continuous joy, living in true obedience to God and His Word, living in harmony with one another, and sowing and reaping to and from one another. There is no lack and no want in faith, and no envy in harmony, but only love working with faith. Women being subject to their husbands allows faith to work, allows hope to manifest, allows prayer to intercede. Men and women have different functions in the workings of God, equal and connected by the Spirit, never a feeling of dominance, one over the other, and no feeling of a need to be equal, except being equal to the task to which God has called us.

Finding our task is easy; we find instruction by Peter in 1 Peter 4:10–11: "Each of you should use whatever gift you have received to serve others, as faithful stewards of God's grace in its various forms." Favor would be a form of God's grace. Grace is unearned favor (kindness, friendly regard, endowed with special grace).

We already have this common gift of faith in us; our quest is to find out what God wants us to do, and *do it*! Ephesians 5:10 says, "Try to find out what is pleasing to the Lord," and do it.

Let us get spiritual; inside ourselves we will find God's perfect plan for our lives. In the Word we will find a passage that excites us a little more than others; we then covet that passage earnestly, and we will operate in the best gifts from God.

God spoke this phrase to my heart, "Spiritual people believe things others only dream of."

Romans 10:10 explains further, "For it is with your heart that you believe and are justified, and it is with your mouth that you profess your faith and are saved." The scripture goes on to say in Romans 10:11, "Anyone who believes in Him will never be put to shame."

So let us covet earnestly these best gifts.

Yet!

Part 2: The Special Gifts of Faith or Special Faith; Given to Supersede Any Natural Happening and Increase Healing Power!

THE GIFT OF SPECIAL FAITH comes after we receive Jesus as our Lord and Savior—an addition to common faith, affording us the opportunity to override nature or natural happenings and be partner to *supernatural* proceedings. The gift of special faith is the greatest of the three power manifestations, ahead of healings and miracles, coming in later chapters.

Brother Howard Carter (author and accredited as a founding father of the Assemblies of God in England) was quoted as saying, "By the gifts of the Spirit we partake of the powers of the world to come, and in a slight, but glorious sense, we experience the functioning of the eternal attributes. By them we can be guided from heaven, in our service for God."

Serving God—serve means to help, to support, to minister to; that is what the gifts are for, to serve God, by serving one another in ministering His precious gifts, one to another.

The gift of special faith can be defined as a supernatural operation of the Holy Spirit, given to us to sustain an unwavering trust in God, for personal protection, and for the provision of our needs. Since this gift is from the Holy Spirit, one would need to be filled with the Holy Spirit to experience any of the gifts of the Spirit. We must have a strong confidence to receive supernatural manifestations and the power to exercise them. The gifts of the Holy Spirit will always magnify the Lord Jesus.

In Genesis 17:5 we see Abram receive a name change from God; God renames him Abraham, which means father of many nations. Down in verse 15 of this same chapter we find Sarai, his wife, also receiving a name change to Sarah, which means princess. God spoke that he would give her a son and that she would be the mother of many nations. I guess we could call Sarah the first princess.

Genesis 17:17 says, "Abraham fell facedown; he laughed and said to himself, Will a son be born to a man a hundred years old? Will Sarah bear a child at the age of ninety?" Genesis 18:10 says, "Then the Lord said, I will surely return to you about this time next year, and Sarah your wife will have a son." Abraham and Sarah were already old and well advanced in years, and Sarah was past the age of childbearing. Abraham was a hundred, and Sarah was ninety years old. But God, who can do all things, produced what He had promised;

they did become the father and mother of many nations, and when we walk by faith, we too are Abraham's offspring. A special gift of faith, God superseded the natural by changing the common age, and the childbearing faculties of Sarah. We know both Abraham and Sarah followed God's plan for this supernatural manifestation of the Holy Spirit because this occurrence is written in Hebrews 11, the faith chapter of the Bible. Hebrews 11:11–12 says, "And by faith even Sarah, who was past childbearing age, was enabled to bear children because she considered Him faithful who had made the promise. And so from this one man, and he as good as dead, came descendants as numerous as the stars in the sky and as countless as the sand on the seashore."

Isaiah says in Isaiah 8:18, "Here am I, and the children the Lord has given me." We are signs and symbols in Israel from the Lord Almighty, who dwells on Mount Zion. Every time we look at our children, or look at ourselves in the mirror, we should see a sign and a wonder of God's promise to Abraham. God's promises are true to all generations, to all who belong to the household of faith.

God sums up what Abraham did and how it pertains to us, now, today in Romans 4:17–21: "As it is written: 'I have made you a father of many nations,' He is our father in the sight of God, in whom he believed—the God who gives life to the dead and calls into being things that were not. Against all hope, Abraham in hope believed and so became the father of many nations, just as it had been said to him, 'So shall your offspring be.' Without weakening in his faith, he faced the fact that his body was as good as dead—since he was about a hundred years old—and that Sarah's womb was also dead. Yet he did not waver through unbelief regarding the promise of God, but was strengthened in his faith and gave glory to God, being fully persuaded that God had power to do what He had promised."

To walk in this common and special faith, it is imperative that we not waver. Wavering is to vacillate between choices, looking at other options. The devil is the author of other options; we need to stay with what God promised. His word is His promise to us; we are Abraham's seed. We must walk by faith, knowing that God is faithful to do what He says. Amen!

As I was driving my mother to a breast cancer treatment center, my two nieces were riding with us to find out my mother's future and possibly theirs. You see, I found out that different generations can be carriers of the disease, so they wanted to know what the tests revealed. While driving I was asking God for a word to raise all our faith, to help my mom be encouraged and to help comfort my nieces, who were not believers. I received the word "Be," followed by "Be localized," "Be shrunk," and "Be eliminated," the breast tumor, that is. I spoke this word to all of us in the van and let them know that God had given us this word to stand on. I wrote this "Be" word down along with a confession for my mother that went like this: "Thank You, God, that this medicine is doing exactly what it was intended to do; I will not get any side effects from this medicine." My mother put this by her bed and would thank God that it was happening, and she read it and said it every night; actually, one of my nieces would remind her. After a period of a couple of months, the tumor was localized and had begun to shrink, praise the Lord. My mother was given a new infused medication, and she did not lose a hair on her head from treatment or medication. On every trip the doctor would tell us more good news, and our faith continued to grow. My mom got back into the Bible and started praying and receiving from God on her own, while my nieces continued with the "Be" word; they even bought "Believe" T-shirts to wear. After a period of a little over a year, my mother had a bone scan, and the results were *all clear*, glory to God. By faith in God's Word and special faith in His leading, we witnessed great results from Jesus, our Healer.

Remember, faith is not baseless; we base our faith on God's Word.

We must have a Bible verse or scripture to solidify our leadings and our proceedings, and we must be doers of the Word of God. God will always keep His Word; He is faithful to His word. Are we?

It takes a righteousness to be given the abilities of faith and to handle and be used in the workings of God. Righteousness is simply right standing with God; let us stay there.

We see a great example in Jesus, the seed of Abraham, sent to show us the kingdom of God and His workings. By a gift of special faith, Jesus raises the daughter of the leader of the synagogue back to life (Matthew 9:24–26). This gift of special faith was also a miracle because the girl was dead, so she did not receive faith by hearing, but Jesus showed the workings of God. He expelled the unbelieving crowd, went to the girl, and took her by the hand, and she arose. Jesus responded to the faith the father had placed in his daughter's life to intercede for her recovery, and by faith in the Master, he went to the Master and asked Him to heal his daughter. We can see a similarity with the ruler and with Abraham and Sarah; they had a common faith that God was able to fulfill what He had promised. Amen!

Many times during His ministry here on earth, Jesus did miracles and special gifts to show the power of God and show that the power of God was present in every generation for producing godlike outcomes. He is still ever present and ever powerful today!

To go further in the common and special gifts of the Holy Spirit, we must include the *anointing*, which is a pouring over of the oil, a representation of the Holy Spirit poured over and in us to do God's bidding in the world and to do it according to His will. The anointing is the unity of God's Word and our hearts, a perceiving into the mysteries and secrets of God, His Spirit, and His ways. Amen!

Psalm 45:7 says, "God your God, has set you above your companions by anointing you with the oil of joy." Joy is a state of well-being, good fortune, and is characterized by gladness or delight. God has joy for us His people, as He stated in Deuteronomy 30:10: "The Lord your God will delight in you if you obey Him." Obedience is the key to receiving anything from God; as we are led by the Spirit of God, we must be doers of that leading.

The *anointing* as found in the Greek means, *"sanctifying grace,"* and is attached to (Khris' mah) the teaching ministry of the Holy Spirit guiding the receptive believer into the fullness of God's preferred will. This power to do God's will, this anointing, functions through faith (pistis); the Greek New Testament defines faith as always being a gift from God, and never something that can be produced by people. True faith, then, would be a common and special gift from God, inwardly persuading us, the believers, of God's preferences. The anointing is a common and a special faith, and a special knowing, a knowing coming from the Word of God, and an inward witness to do the Word, which comes from hearing.

The gift of faith in operation brings the invisible and limitless resources of heaven to us, giving us an extraordinary faith and the protection of angels. When provision is required, it may come by birds or by a never-failing barrel of meal. In 1 Kings 17 we read about a drought coming on for the next three years; *at God's Word*, Elijah will be well provided for, but he must go where God is sending him. First Kings 17:2–4 says, "Then the Word of the Lord came to Elijah: 'Leave here, turn eastward and hide in the Kerith Ravine, east of the Jordan. You will drink from the brook, and I have directed the ravens to supply you with food there.' Elijah went where God sent him, and he was richly provided for. What faith he had, to first go where God sent him, and then to wait for the ravens to provide for him. Can you imagine these birds flying to get Elijah's provision, and not eating it? The ravens were sent to perform a task that would provide for the man of God and would show God faithful! Wow, what an awesome display of God's faithfulness. What God had spoken earlier to Elijah in this seventeenth chapter was also happening to the brook Kerith; it was drying up for lack of rain. Now what? Elijah was in his place of provision and prosperity, but the brook was now dried up. But before he could doubt, the Word of the Lord came to him, saying, "Go at once to Zarephath in the region of Sidon and stay there. I have directed a widow there to supply you with food." God at the brook commanded a raven; here God commands a widow woman. Our faith must fall in line with His commands (a command is to exercise a dominating influence over). God was influencing a raven and then a widow; both followed God's commands, and miracles happened; I wonder if that works for us today? The answer to that question is yes! We have the same Provider, the same Commander; we have an added Gift and His name is the Holy Spirit, our Helper, Comforter, and ever-present inner Commander. Amen!

For us to operate by faith at any level we must be obedient, and our obedience is in direct relation to our trust in God, which actually is faith at an elevated level. Obedient people are doers, and doers get—the provision, the food and water in a drought, the miracles—all these gifts of God come by being a great hearer, and a quick-to-do doer.

We read in 1 Kings 17:12 the widow lady was ready to make herself and her son their last meal, and then she had planned their death. "I am gathering a few sticks to take home and make a meal for myself and my son that we may eat it—and die." Elijah said to her, "Don't be afraid. Go home and do as you have said. But first make a small loaf of bread for me from what you have and bring it to me, and then make something for yourself and your son. For this is what the Lord, the God of Israel, says: 'The jar of flour will not be used up, and the jug of oil will not run dry until the day the Lord sends rain on the land.' By following the Lord's commands and taking a step of faith, supernatural provision was happening; remember the widow and the raven were commanded by God to meet the man of God's needs.

Has God commanded you to give, or make, or sow anything? For the gifts of the Holy Spirit to be in operation in our lives, we must do *all* that we have been commanded. Jesus' mother said it best in John 2:5: "Do whatever He tells you." All the great workings of God happen at this point. We have a choice to make, every time we arrive at this point. We know what He said; we have a witness from the Holy Spirit. Now it is time to do, and the doers of the commands get the miracles.

We must remember that all our faith and doings must honor and bring glory to God; we are not to be faith giants to show our spirituality but to show our God's great power and abilities in and to us, His people. We really are His pearl of great price. How does the gift of faith bring glory to God? Since faith pleases God, the gift of special faith must elate Him. Through this gift we can overcome all the powers and forces that would come against us, whether natural or spiritual. Faith working through love is connected to the greatest power ever, and our believing allows all things to be possible. We see the words of Jesus in Mark 9:23: "Everything is possible for one who believes."

My spiritual father in the faith once told a brother in the faith of a great item he was believing for; it seemed too lofty at the present time. I will never forget this faithful brother's response: "You can have anything you can believe for." What an encouraging word. My question to you today is, what are you believing for?

We must remember that "faith is the substance of things hoped for, the evidence of things not seen" (Hebrews 11:1). Faith has a base, and that base is the Word of God. Faith, in the Greek, is isotimos, which means having the same or equal value, and is only used in 2 Peter 1:1: "To those who through the righteousness of our God and Savior Jesus Christ have received a faith as precious as ours." A like precious faith (isotimos pistis), conveys that every faith decision and/or action has equal, eternal value, so let us covet earnestly these best gifts.

Yet!

CHAPTER 5

Common and Special Gifts of the Working of Miracles
A natural and supernatural power to
produce signs and wonders

Part 1: The Common Gift of Miracles Includes Seed Time, and Harvest, Ocean Tide, Child Conception, and Childbirth

WE WILL FIRST DISTINGUISH MIRACLES from healings. Miracles are supernatural demonstrations of God's power by which the Laws of Nature are altered, suspended, or controlled by God's invention or intervention. *Miracles* demonstrate the power of God, and *healings* demonstrate His love and compassion. The Holy Spirit gives both (the power and the love) to His believers at His willing, sometimes working together but not overlapping.

The miracle of seed time and harvest is found in Mark 4:26–29: "He also said, 'this is what the kingdom of God *is like*. A man scatters seed on the ground. Night and day, whether he sleeps or gets up, the seed sprouts and grows, though he does not know how.' All by itself the soil produces grain—first the stalk, then the head, then the full kernel in the head. As soon as the grain is ripe, he puts the sickle to it, because the harvest has come." Jesus said that the kingdom is like sowing and reaping, the *time* from the sowing to the reaping is the miraculous part, God's part. In this passage Jesus states, "He does not know how." He is talking about the man. The man scatters seed, good seed; God controls the growth elements (faith, patience, perseverance, water, sunlight etc.). We, the man, must trust that God will and is doing His part; if we dig up the seed, we will never have a harvest. We don't need to know God's part; we need to trust that God will do what He says He will do. Amen! We do have a part to play in all happenings of God in our life and, when He calls on us, in the lives of others. We can use what are considered natural items and processes to experience supernatural results and happenings.

In Judges 14:5–6, we see Samson walking in a common gift of miracles; as Samson and his father and mother were approaching Timnah (in verse 5), a young lion came roaring toward him. The Spirit of the Lord came powerfully upon him, so that he tore the lion apart with his bare hands, as he might have torn a young goat. The Spirit of God gave Samson, an already strong man, more power by coming upon him mightily, as we read; this lion slaying was performed with seemingly little effort. God's power affords us strength and abilities far greater than any natural beast.

Sometimes we look past the real miracle, and that is what God was able to do because of the miracle. Verses 8 and 9 of this same chapter say, "Sometime later, when he went back to marry her, he turned aside to look at the lion's carcass, and in it he saw a swarm of bees and some honey. He scooped out the honey with his hands and ate as he went along." This provisional miracle came out of Samson receiving the power of God. Samson went on to speak a riddle in verse 14, and he said to them, "Out of the eater, something to eat; out of the strong, something sweet." In verse 18 the riddle is solved, and it is what we would think. What is sweeter than honey? What is stronger than a lion? Supernatural strength and sweetness that is our God, our provider, our miracle producer!

As we look at another of these great *common*, spectacular miracles, we see one of the most talked about and quoted miracles of all time, Moses and the Red Sea. In Exodus 14:15–18 we see what the Lord said to Moses. "Why are you crying out to me? Tell the Israelites to move on! Raise your staff and stretch out your hand over the sea to divide the water so that the Israelites can go through the sea on dry ground. (Faith is the common denominator.) I will harden the hearts of the Egyptians so that they will go in after them. And I will gain glory through Pharaoh and all his army, through the chariots and his horsemen. (God will cause the Egyptians to think they can walk in the Israelites' faith.) The Egyptians will know that I am the Lord when I gain glory through Pharaoh, his chariots and his horsemen." Let us read further to see the greater, or special, miracle that takes place. Exodus 14:26–28 says, "The Lord said to Moses, 'Stretch out your hand over the sea so that the waters may flow back over the Egyptians and their chariots and horsemen.' Moses stretched out his hand over the sea, and at daybreak the sea went back to its place. The Egyptians were fleeing toward it, and the Lord swept them into the sea. The water flowed back and covered the chariots and horsemen—the entire army of Pharaoh that had followed the Israelites into the sea. Not one of them survived."

The greater part of this widely quoted passage is that Moses was still paying close attention to God on the other side, and what transpired on the other side is what God wanted—all of Egypt to know that He was the only God.

Staying with God during and after the victory shows that we have the faith to hold onto a miracle from God. God has provided many daily miracles for us to walk in and have participation in; let us covet earnestly these best gifts!

When we look at and experience the miracles of God, we also need to look at the principles of God. The creating principle of God is *wisdom*. God said this is so in Proverbs 4:5–7: "Get wisdom, get understanding; do not forget My words or turn away from them. Do not forsake wisdom, and she will protect you; love her, and she will watch over you. The beginning of wisdom is this: Get wisdom. Though it cost all you have, get understanding." Verses 20–23 say, "My son, pay attention to what I say; turn your ear to My words. Do not let them out of your sight, keep them within your heart; for they are life to those who find them and health to one's whole body. Above all else, guard your heart, for everything you do flows from it."

We can never discover God's great powers as found in the gifts of the Spirit, independent of His workings, His creativity, and His creation. We need to connect our heart to God's heart and guard it with all we have. Wisdom was God's architect as He was forming and fashioning the world, and all His creation! Wisdom as the architect is found in Proverbs 8:22–31: "The Lord brought me forth as the first of His works, before His deeds of old; I was formed long ages ago, at the very beginning, when the world came to be. When there were no watery depths, I was given birth, when there were no springs overflowing with water; before the mountains were settled in place, before the hills, I was given birth, before He made the world or its fields or any of the dust of the earth. I was there when He set the heavens in place, when He marked the horizon on the face of the deep, when He established the clouds above and fixed securely the fountains of the deep, when He gave the sea its boundary so the waters would not overstep His command, and when He marked out the foundations of the earth. Then I was constantly at His side. I was filled with delight day after day, rejoicing always in His presence, rejoicing in His whole world and delighting in mankind." Wisdom is a creator, not a debater; wisdom is Jesus! Something stands out in verse 23: "appointed from eternity" (eternity—appointed from an infinite time, or span of time). We usually see eternity as our future; in this passage eternity is also the basis of our beginning. Amen!

We truly are spiritual people of a spiritual God; as He is, so are we; we "were"; we "are," and we will forever "be," glory to God. Talk about miraculous, our eternal life started before we were; before we ever breathed a breath, we were. He formed us in His realm and in His image. We were, and are, formed and fashioned by a design that cannot fail. We see God's Word on this in Jeremiah 1:5: "Before I formed you in the womb I knew you; before you were born I set you apart." It seems very likely that we were formed by the dust He talks about in Proverbs 8:26. I am grateful for a creating God, thankful that He saw me before I was, loved me through the rebellious times, and allows me full companionship and participation with His Son Jesus Christ, today.

Friend, do you know Him? He knows and understands you.

The realization of conception and childbirth is rather natural, although many times throughout the Bible, God shows Himself strong by adding His power to and altering what we consider the normal way and time of conception.

Each occurrence when God intervenes, He is always keeping His Word and promises.

Luke 1:11–17 says, "Then an angel of the Lord appeared to him (Zechariah), standing at the right side of the altar of incense. When Zechariah saw him, he was startled and was gripped with fear. But the angel said to him: 'Do not be afraid, Zechariah; your prayer has been heard. Your wife Elizabeth will bear you a son, and you are to call him John. He will be a joy and delight to you, and many will rejoice because of his birth, for he will be great in the sight of the

Lord. He is never to take wine or other fermented drink, and he will be filled with the Holy Spirit even before he is born. (This verse lines up with our eternity being from before we were). He will bring back many of the people of Israel to the Lord their God. And he will go on before the Lord, in the spirit and power of Elijah, to turn the hearts of the parents to their children and the disobedient to the wisdom of the righteous—to make ready a people prepared for the Lord' In verses 23–34 we see that when his time of service was completed, he returned home. After this, his wife Elizabeth became pregnant and for five months remained in seclusion. "The Lord has done this for me," she said. This was a common gift of the Spirit increased by the grace of God. As we go further in this passage we see the same angel, Gabriel, come to Mary (the highly favored of the Lord), the soon-to-be mother of Jesus, and present a special gift of miracles to her. Gabriel in verse 31 says, "You will conceive and give birth to a son, and you are to call him Jesus. He will be great and will be called the Son of the Most High. The Lord God will give Him the throne of His father David and He will reign over Jacob's descendants forever; His kingdom will never end" (an eternal kingdom). Mary asks a question in verse 34 that is not doubting but wondering (there is a difference in wondering how God will do things, and doubting if God will do things). Back in verse 18, Zechariah asked the angel, "How can I be sure of this?" This questions God's character. Gabriel had already told him that the Lord had sent him; he should have found his surety in that. The gift of the birth of John was an answer to Zechariah's prayer, the Bible says.

When we ask of the Lord and believe we receive, we must have a willingness to receive. When we ask God big things, we should be expecting and willing and/or trusting in God to produce and provide big things. Our receiving ability is in direct relation to what God can do for us, by our faith—believing, we receive. When our faith becomes substance, we must possess what we believed for. Lay hold of the promises, seize the desires, *and realize the wonders.*

He is worthy to provide much more than we can ask or imagine by and through His Son Jesus. Ephesians 3:20 tells us this truth: "Now to Him who is able to do immeasurably more than all we ask or imagine, according to His power that is at work within us."

Jesus is everything; let us covet earnestly the best gifts.

Yet!

Part 2: The Special Gift of Miracles— the Altering of the Natural by Miraculous Intervention, Causing Godly Outcomes

SPECIAL MIRACLES ARE A DEFINITE sign of the power of God and the presence of God. They bring results instantly when results look unattainable; they provide when provision is nonexistent. Special miracles would also at times reveal a divine commission. Amen!

When God spoke of coveting earnestly these best gifts, He knew we would need a strong desire to see His power in our world. The reason we do not see miracles abounding in our lives is in direct relation to our earnest desire.

Jesus said in Luke 18:8, "I tell you, he will see that they get justice, and quickly. However, when the Son of Man comes, will He find faith on the earth?" All the gifts of the Spirit require faith, so if we are living in a time or season of spiritual declension, we should elevate our Word time. We must keep our believing in line with God's Word, what He said. Faith must be activated to receive a miracle, not necessarily special faith, but faith even as a mustard seed can bring a great miracle.

When I was a grade school lad I was thrown under a tractor by its rear tire, and then the opposite tire severed my foot, which was hanging only by the skin on one side. This disaster started the miracle process that I walked out over a course of time; first there was a specialist that happened to be at the small hospital to which I was transported. After four hours of surgery, my foot was reattached. That was the beginning of the restoration powers of God that I would realize at a very early age—the possibility of no use of that leg, the possibility of no further growth of that leg, all the medical facts being what they were. But God had a different plan. You see, right when this accident happened, my uncle, a minister of the gospel, went to the house, grabbed all my relatives who were present, and prayed! He prayed for the miracle-working power of the Most High God, to overshadow this seemingly tragic accident. My uncle taught me to believe for a miracle, I fought hard, worked long hours at rehabilitation, and was always prayed for by my mother and many other family members. My leg continued to grow as normal; my development continued after a long motionless state that my entire leg had to be in to promote this healing process.

Then the miracle took place, not all of a sudden, but all of a sudden I was walking without a limp. I could keep up with other kids on the ball field, and weight started falling off as I was able to become more and more active. After a period of twenty years, as I was having some foot pain, a podiatrist took some x-rays of my previously severed foot. He came back into the room astounded. He stated, "It is a miracle that you can walk; your anklebones and attaching bones look as if your walking would be impossible." He then asked if he could keep the x-rays to show his brother, also a podiatrist.

The word impossible is not in the vocabulary of a child of God; we believe and then we receive salvation, prosperity, and miracle-working power. Amen!

Jesus walked in the special gifts of miracles in response to needed provision, as well as healing and the casting out of demons, or evil spirits. We see this in John 6:5–14: "When Jesus looked up and saw a great crowd coming toward Him, He said to Phillip, 'Where shall we buy bread for these people to eat?'" He was testing Philip, for He already knew what He was going to do. He already *knew*. It must be possible that as the need was coming toward Jesus He knew from that inner witness, the Holy Spirit rising up in Him, what to do. We have this same ability in us—the ability to know when and how to apply God's miraculous power into any situation no matter how large or what the need is.

Wonder-working power is available to all who choose to believe and walk in it, and apply it by faith; remember, *faith is* the confidence in what we hope for and assurance about what we do not see (Hebrews 11:1).

Jesus, in John 6, had the evidence working in Him to will and do what the Holy Spirit gave Him ahead of time, the knowing of what to do.

Let's read on, in verses 7–12: "Phillip answered Him, it would take more than half a year's wages to buy enough bread for each one to have a bite!" Another of His disciples, Andrew, Simon Peter's brother, spoke up, "Here is a boy with five small barley loaves and two small fish, but how far will they go among so many?" (Andrew saw the *seed* for the miracle, but did not have a knowing or the faith to apply it.) Jesus said, "Have the people sit down." Plenty of grass was in that place, and they sat down (about five thousand men were there). Jesus then took the loaves, gave thanks, and distributed to those who were seated as much as they wanted. He did the same with the fish. When they all had enough to eat, He said to His disciples, "Gather up the pieces that are left over. Let nothing be wasted."

This was a special gift of miracles—abundant provision with leftovers, coming out of a seed. Amen!

A wonderful part of this passage is the young boy being in the right place at the right time, having an offering and willing to give all he had. The boy's name is not mentioned here, but I am confident he has a place in the Master's stead.

As we continue on in John 6, we see Jesus walking on the water (miracle), and Jesus tells us about Him being the Bread of Life. John 6:25–29 says, "When they found Him on the other side of the lake, they asked him, 'Rabbi, when did you get here?'" Jesus answered, "Very truly I tell you, you are looking for me, not because you saw the signs I performed but because you ate the loaves and had your fill. Do not work for food that spoils, but for food that endures to eternal life, which the Son of Man will give you. For on Him God the Father has placed His seal of approval." Then they asked Him, "What must we do to do the works God requires?" Jesus answered, "The work of God is this: to believe in the One He has sent." Believe in the One He has sent, not because we have seen Him but, more importantly, because we believe and have not seen Him, but also love Him. We see confirmation to this truth in John 20:29–31: 'Then Jesus told him, 'Because you have seen Me, you have believed; blessed are those who have not seen and yet have believed.'

Jesus did many other miraculous signs in the presence of His disciples, which are not recorded in this book. But these are written that you may believe (and continue to believe, as a side note) that Jesus is the Christ, the Son of God, and that by believing you may have life in His name. Life in His name; the name of Jesus brings eternal life. As we read in John 6:27, we must spend our spiritual energy in the Word of God, seeking, believing, loving, and doing His plan and will for us who believe.

Eternal life is not only a future, but a very real past and present; we through Jesus have the ability to know where we have come from, where we are, and, yes, where we will spend our future.

Where we have been, we have memory of! Selah!

We by believing in and on Jesus can achieve a knowing of our Creator, our God who sent us, who thought of us before we were, loved us in this sin-fallen world, and has received us back to Glory through His Son Jesus Christ. Amen! Do you believe?

Read through Matthew, Mark, Luke, and John to see all of Jesus' miracles, given to alter and control godly outcomes in many situations, but always bringing glory to the Father. These miracles continue after Jesus suffered crucifixion, perished, rose from the dead, and sent His Holy Spirit to all of us believers, starting with the eleven and those waiting patiently in the upper room. Luke 24:49 says, "I am going to send you what my Father has promised; but stay in the city until you have been clothed with power from on high." The Holy Spirit of His Son, Jesus. Amen! In John 20:22 we see this giving of the Spirit again: "And with that He breathed on them and said, 'Receive the Holy Spirit.' He, the Holy Spirit, is the power to will and do God's will. Amen! The book after the four gospels starts the ministering of the gifts of the Spirit, through the church, through the apostles, for the people and for all time—the acts of the Holy Spirit through the church, or the Acts of the Apostles.

We begin with a special gift of miracles, in Acts 1:6–7. Then they gathered around Him and asked Him, "Lord, are you at this time going to restore the kingdom to Israel?" He said to them: "It is not for you to know the times or dates the Father has set by His own authority. But you will receive power when the Holy Spirit comes on you; and you will be my witnesses in Jerusalem, and in all Judea and Samaria, and to the ends of the earth."

Many times we hear from different religious sects and ministers that the end is coming; some think they know the end from the beginning, but the scripture above says not true. Jesus said that we do not need to know the time and that only the Father knows this, but our function here on this planet is to be filled with the Holy Spirit to overflowing, to do good deeds, and to be a witness for Jesus to the ends of the earth. An excellent example of a good witness is Jesus Himself. He only said what He heard the Father saying, and He only did what He saw the Father doing. God is a Spirit; He communicates to us through our spirit, which originated in Him. Amen!

Gifts of special miracles come up out of our spirit, and are controlled by God via His Holy Spirit given liberally to us all.

We see a very real, ever-present denominator to receiving the Spirit of God. In Acts 2, Peter was questioned by the people on what they could do to be saved and receive the gift of the Holy Spirit. He replied, "REPENT and be baptized, every one of you, in the name of Jesus Christ for the forgiveness of your sins. And you *will* receive the gift of the Holy Spirit" (Acts 2:38).

Repent means to make a moral U-turn from sin, to God, and have a changed heart and behavior. Repentance is necessary to receive anything from God—salvation, provision, and, most importantly, His Holy Spirit.

God sends His orders to the world by His Spirit, and we, having that same spirit of faith, can receive and minister the gifts of the Spirit to people and situations.

Further into the book of Acts we find Peter traveling and ministering the gifts of the Holy Spirit. In Acts 9:32–42, we see two miraculous workings, first a special miracle of healing, and second a special miracle of raising the dead.

As we see in Acts 9:31, the churches are strengthened and encouraged by the Holy Spirit and by living in the fear of the Lord. This reverence is a necessity to receive any and all gifts of the Holy Spirit; the leaders and believers can and should operate in one or a combination of many of these gifts.

Let us read on in verses 32–35: "As Peter traveled about the country, he went to visit the Lord's people who lived in Lydda. There he found a man named Aeneas, who was paralyzed and had been bedridden for eight years. 'Aeneas,' Peter said to him, 'Jesus Christ heals you. Get up and roll up your mat.' Immediately Aeneas got up. All those who lived in Lydda and Sharon saw him and turned to the Lord." Peter was doing what he saw the Master do; he was doing what Jesus had commissioned him to do. Amen! These doings are available today; we are part of the same church that started in Acts. We have the same strengthening, the same encouragement, and the same Holy Spirit working in us to will and do God's will. Let us covet earnestly these best gifts.

In Acts 9:36–40, we see Peter continuing on to Joppa, and there was a disciple named Tabitha (which means Dorcas). She was always doing good and helping the poor. About that time she became sick and died, and her body was washed and placed in an upstairs room. Lydda was near Joppa; so when the disciples heard that Peter was in Lydda, they sent two men to him and urged him, "Please come at once!" Peter went with them, and when he arrived he was taken upstairs to the room. All the widows stood around him, crying and showing him the robes and other clothing that Dorcas had made while she was still with them. Peter sent them all out of the room; then he got down on his knees and prayed. Turning toward the dead woman, he said, "Tabitha, get up." She opened her eyes, and seeing Peter, she sat up. He took her by the hand and helped her to her feet. Then he called for the believers, especially the widows, and presented her to them alive. This became known all over Joppa, and many people believed in the Lord.

Is it still necessary to humble yourself? Peter got down on his knees to inquire of the Lord, to get his instructions. He removed the unbelief from the room. As we see in verse 41; he called the believers and the widows back into the room; we see a separation between the ones who came believing with Peter to raise her up, and the ones crying and already mourning. These are both special gifts of miracles; God intervened and caused spectacular outcomes. We do see reverence in these miracles; we also see belief in these miracles. The end result is that God received the glory, and men turned to Him. Amen! As with all the workings and doings of God, in and through us, we must *believe*. Our faith in God and His Holy Spirit enables us to perceive and do mighty workings.

In Acts 12:1–9 we see the special gifts of miracles at work on an inanimate object. We read that Peter was arrested, thrown into prison, heavily guarded, and bound with chains. In verse 7 we see an angel of the Lord appear to Peter and say, "Wrap your cloak around you and follow me." So he went out and followed him (the angel of the Lord), and did not know if what was being done by the angel was real (he couldn't tell), but thought he was seeing a vision. When they were past the first and second guard posts, they came to the iron gate that led to the city, *which opened to them on its own accord*; this was a special miracle, and as we read on we see Peter pondering on the situation, coming to a conclusion that the Lord sent His angel and delivered Peter from the hand of Herod.

We see many workings in this special gift of miracles. In verse 5 we see the church praying for him constantly, prompting God to send Peter an angel (a real spiritual being, seen by and in light). We see all of Peter's bindings falling off; we see him pass guard posts without being seen, and a gate, an iron gate that opened on its own accord. Amazing! God's power was working in and through the church, in and through the faithful, and producing spectacular outcomes, expected and received. That's *faith*! Amen!

Faith working in and through the church and one another; that's how God set the church up in Acts 2, and that is still the way it works today. We believe on His Son Jesus, we speak our belief out of a pure heart; we are filled with the Holy Spirit. We petition God; we stand in faith; we believe we receive, and we expectantly wait until. "Until when?" you might ask. Until you receive your asking, receive your bindings removed, and receive your miracle, for you or another.

Revelation 1:5 says, "And from Jesus Christ, who is the faithful witness, the firstborn from the dead and the Ruler of the kings of the earth. To Him who loves us and has freed us from our sins by His blood."

Let us covet earnestly these best gifts.

Yet!

CHAPTER 6

Common and Special Gifts of Healing
A natural and supernatural power, given by
God, to remove disease and infirmities

Part 1: The Common Gifts of Healing—Our Body's Power, Created by and in God, to Eliminate Non-Life-Threatening Diseases, Cuts, and Contusions

GOD HAS PLACED IN EACH one of us a healing power; it works without our faith and actions. It truly is spectacular in essence but does not necessarily need our faith, as a supernatural healing would require. Our bodies are fearfully and wonderfully made. Amen!

Look at Psalm 139:13–16: "For You created my inmost being; You knit me together in my mother's womb. I praise You because I am fearfully and wonderfully made; Your works are wonderful, I know that full well. My frame was not hidden from You when I was made in the secret place, when I was woven together in the depths of the earth. Your eyes saw my unformed body; all the days ordained for me were written in Your book before one of them came to be." Not only are we fearfully and wonderfully made, He knows what we are made of and what He planned for us. *Healing* is in His plan; our body has the ability to heal itself. What an amazing creation are we!

In the above passage God speaks of ordaining us. Ordain means: (a) to invest officially by the laying on of hands, with ministerial or priestly authority; (b) to determine the fate of in advance. God laid His hands on our lives before we ever lived a day; He has given us the authority over our bodies and every choice we make. He has determined a course for us to take; that course is free from any hurts or diseases, but we live in a curse-filled, sin-filled world, so there are times our bodies need to be healed. At these times your body's godly powers kick in to get your body back on track with the book He wrote about you. God did not write about diseases for you in His book. His plan for us is to be and stay whole. Amen!

Remember, we are spirits; we live in a body, and we have a soul.

We always hear about health or healthy. I find God's definition of this in Mark 5: 34 and it is the best explanation of staying healed or healthy: "Daughter, your faith has healed you. Go in peace and be freed from your suffering." Health is the art of staying healed, free from distress and disease, as stated in the verse we just read. Our God gave us the ability to walk in health our entire lives; the key word is "gave us," and we have a big part to play.

When we know what to change, what to start, or what to stop— eating, doing, participating in—our choices will have a great bearing on how healthy we stay. We need to keep a clear conscience on eating and exercise choices, as well as on spiritual choices, for they are connected.

Remember, we are a spirit; we live in a body, and we have a soul.

God calls this body we possess a temple, "His temple." In 1 Corinthians 6:19–20, we see this: "Or do you not know that your body is the temple of the Holy Spirit who is in you, whom you have from God, and you are not your own. For you were bought with a price; therefore glorify God in your body and in your spirit, which are God's." Making wrong choices with this body God has given us equates to sin, and sin always has loss attached to it. Read verses 17 and 18 of the above passage. Since we are not our own and have been bought with the highest price that can be paid for us, let us covet earnestly our God-given ability to keep our bodies healthy.

Jesus paid the full ransom for us to walk in freedom; in Psalm 111:9 we see this: "He provided redemption for His people; He ordained His covenant forever—holy and awesome is His name." There is nothing left to be paid, just received. Amen! We must receive leadings from our God-given spirit; we must heed wise counsel; we must receive correction to stay healed. Healed people live a full life and achieve all God's purpose and plan—that plan He wrote about your days before you lived even one. What an awesome Creator we have!

Reverencing the Lord is the foundation of true wisdom. The rewards of wisdom come to all who obey Him (Psalm 111:10). The rewards of wisdom are: long life in one hand, and riches and honor in the other hand of God. This truth is found in Proverbs 3:16.

If we base our lives on the Word of God, we will always have the remedy before the complaint. Amen!

Let us covet earnestly the best gifts.

Yet!

Part 2: The Special Gifts of Healing— Increased Power to Heal, at a Supernatural Speed, and Spiritual Intervention. The Cause and Effect of Faith!

WE WILL FIRST DEFINE CAUSE and effect. *Cause* is: (a) something that brings about an effect or result, (b) a factor. *Effect* is: (a) a condition or occurrence traceable to a cause, (b) an outward sign, (c) power bringing about a result.

As a result of our faith, we receive Jesus and His Holy Spirit that He left us to be our only source of life and light. The effect of this believing and receiving is gifts of the Holy Spirit, given as He wills.

Healing is a very significant part of this giving. The special gift of healing comes from God. God ordained and gave His Son Jesus this special power; Jesus still uses that power today through His Holy Spirit, which is in us who receive Him. Amen! Our Helper, Healer, Comforter, our spirit in us connects with the Holy Spirit, becomes one with and is in tune with the Holy Spirit, and we receive the power to overcome anything. As we walk in tune with, accordance with, conforming to the Holy Spirit and His leadings, we become more and more aware of the ministering powers afforded us in Him. Romans 8:5 says, "Those who live according to the sinful nature have their minds set on what that nature desires, but those who live in accordance (in tune) with the Spirit have their minds set on what the Spirit desires."

We receive and minister special gifts of healings; to receive from the supernatural, we must keep our minds set on the supernatural, live in tune with our spirits, and be ye led by the Holy Spirit. In doing the leadings of the Holy Spirit, we will see great gifts of healings as well as all the other manifestations of the Spirit in operation.

In a recent trip to my doctor for a physical, I was told I needed to see a dermatologist for some skin issues on my shoulders, back, and chest. At the dermatologist's visit, I was told multiple times that I had skin cancer. As he pointed out six different spots, he kept exclaiming, "That's cancer." To my surprise, nothing the doctor said moved me; I was confident in my Healer, and I know my Healer is Jesus. I had biopsies and, just as he had said, all six were some form of basal cell carcinoma; four needed cream treatment, and two needed to be removed through surgery. I went to a surgeon, and as he was telling me what he was going to do, I knew I should not be there (I just knew). So after leaving his office, I phoned back and explained that I would not be having surgery. I had a knowing that I was healed and knew a healing was taking place. I had a leading from the Holy Spirit, and I followed this leading back to the dermatologist. He looked again at all six carcinomas and stated that he was pleased with the way they all looked. You see, I had put the prescribed cream on the four not needing surgery. He said, "Let's try the cream on the two other severe carcinomas, and forget about the surgery." Well, God had led me right into a healing; at my next visit I was told the wonderful words "all clear." God is faithful. Amen!

We see another way to stay in tune with our spirit in Galatians 5:25: "Since we live by the Spirit, let us keep in step with the Spirit." Always doing right when we know to do it keeps us in tune with the Spirit. Keeping a clear conscience keeps us in step with the Holy Spirit and also allows us the ability to be comforted and to comfort others, thus fulfilling the love command. Jesus said in John 13:34: "A new command I give you: Love one another. As I have loved you, so you must love one another." Amen! When operating in the gifts of the Holy Spirit, two principles will and must be present, *faith and love*, faith working through love.

The special gifts of healings are: A spiritual and supernatural manifestation of the Holy Ghost given to the church for the purpose of removing sickness, disease, and infirmity. (From brother Howard Carter's definition as found in his book *Questions and Answers on Spiritual Gifts*.)

Let us look at some examples in the Bible. In Genesis 20:17 we see an early special gift of healing when Abraham prayed, and God healed. "Then Abraham prayed to God, and God healed Abimelech, his wife and his slave girls." This gift was in tune with a prayer; God still answers prayer today. Amen!

In 2 Kings 5:1–19 we see Naaman, a mighty warrior who had leprosy, was informed of a prophet in Samaria by his wife's maid and was told he would be healed of his leprosy if he visited the prophet. Namaan went to Samaria and was expecting his miraculous healing to come *his way*, calling down angels to minister to him, causing lightning to flash, or God Himself coming down to touch him. When he got to the prophet Elisha, Elisha did not even come out to greet him. He sent his messenger with this message, found in 2 Kings 5:10: "Go, wash yourself seven times in the Jordan, and your flesh will be restored, and you will be cleansed." But Namaan became angry and stalked away. "I thought he would surely come out to meet me!" he said. "I expected him to wave his hand over the leprosy and call on the name of the Lord his God to heal me." Namaan was not even open to the river the prophet picked and went away in a rage. Then his officers reasoned with him and said, as recorded in verse 13, "Sir if the prophet had told you to do some great thing, wouldn't you have done it? So you should certainly obey him when he says simply to go and wash and be cured! So Namaan went down to the Jordan River and dipped himself seven times, as the man of God had instructed him. And his flesh became as healthy as a young child's, and he was healed." A true special gift of healing, it brought glory and honor to God, and showed His prophet true. A measure of faith was not what produced this healing; it did not come by hearing. It came to show that God was present to heal and that men still heard from Him and could instruct others as to His biddings.

One of the greatest traits needed for a gift of healing is openness, a willingness to remove ourselves and place our faith in God's way. His ways are much higher than our ways; His thoughts are much higher than our thoughts. It takes ongoing faith to receive and keep a special gift of healing, and thus we must humble ourselves to receive from God. Amen! Faith comes by hearing and provides many gifts, including healing. It takes humility to receive special gifts of healing, as we see in this story of Namaan. All the workings of God will and must bring glory to God. He alone is worthy.

In Matthew 8:8–13, the centurion replied, "Lord, I do not deserve to have you come under my roof. But just say the word, and my servant will be healed. For I myself am a man under authority, with soldiers under me. I tell this one, 'Go,' and he goes; and that one, 'Come,' and he comes. I say to my servant, 'Do this,' and he does it." When Jesus heard this, He was amazed and said to those following him, "Truly I tell you, I have not found anyone in Israel with such great faith. I say to you that many will come from the east and the west, and will take their places at the feast with Abraham, Isaac, and Jacob in the kingdom of heaven. But the subjects of the kingdom will be thrown outside into the darkness, where there will be weeping and gnashing of teeth." Then Jesus said to the centurion, "Go! Let it be done just as you believed it would." And His servant was healed at that moment.

The centurion's honor of Jesus and who Jesus was and what He was able to do, his regard to authority, and his submission to it not only moved Jesus to heal the centurion's servant (as we read the rest of the passage), but Jesus also marveled at his faith.

Every time that Jesus' own disciples failed to respond in the correct manner to winds and waves, to speaking things into existence and believing, and to casting out demons, He always reproved them because of and in relation to their faith, or actually lack of faith. ("Where's your faith? Oh you of little faith!") Is it possible that His disciples at times were not as honorable as the centurion? Is it possible that even when those who are close to God have pride in their relationship with God, that a soldier gets more results? The centurion's understanding of honor and submission caused a special gift of healing to be given to his servant. It is remarkable that when honor is present (our honoring God and the things of God), Jesus sees this as marvelous faith. He recorded it here so that we could see it for all time. Amen! Let our honoring God and our faith in God bring healing into our sphere, transferred from the heavenly realm to ours.

The special gifts of healing are manifested (realized) through many natural elements: the laying on of hands in Mark 6:5, the spoken Word in Matthew 8:8, a common fabric in Acts 9:11–12, and even by a shadow found in Acts 5:15–16. This passage starts out with the phrase "as a result." This result was in reference to the reverential fear of the Lord, a respect for the Holy Ghost, and what happened when the Holy Spirit was lied to (read verses 1–14). In verse 15 we read that as a result, people brought the sick into the streets and laid them on beds and mats so that at least Peter's shadow might fall on some of them as he passed by. Crowds gathered also from the towns around Jerusalem, bringing their sick and those tormented by evil spirits, and all of them were healed. "All of them were healed"—past tense. "All of them were healed." Selah! (Pause and think about that.)

Peter's honor of Jesus and what Jesus told His followers to do (wait till the Holy Spirit comes on you) before His ascension into heaven, made him just like Jesus. In many of the gospel accounts, we see: Jesus healing them all, Luke 4:40; He healed many, Mark 1:34; and Jesus healed all who needed healing, Luke 9:11. Jesus was and still is the Healer. He needs our hands now; He needs our voice now; He needs our heart now, and we must become His doers in the earth. Amen!

We have the same Holy Spirit today, and the gifts of the Holy Spirit are still given to those doing the works of Jesus, doing His bidding on the earth. Greater things than these shall we see! Jesus said this in John 14:12, "Very truly I tell you, whoever believes in Me will do the works I have been doing, and they will do even greater things than these, because I am going to the Father."

The faithful truly are the doers of the Word and the works of Jesus. What an awesome Spirit He left us. Let us therefore live a life full of light, God's Light; full of healings; and full of the common and special gifts of the Holy Spirit! Amen! John 1:9 says, "The true light that gives light to everyone was coming into the world."

We must covet earnestly these best gifts.

Yet!

THE GIFTS OF ENCOURAGEMENT

CHAPTER 7

Common and Special Gifts of Prophecy
A natural and supernatural utterance,
inspired by God, in a known tongue

**Part 1: The Common Gift of Prophecy: A Spoken
Revelation Given from the Word of God, and in Line
with the Word of God, to Us Who Believe, and as
a Means to Encourage Like Believers. Amen!**

A PROPHECY IS OR CAN be a sudden inspiration to speak; this speaking
comes from the light of God's Word. A common prophecy can be very
fundamental and enlightening for the now, or for predicting future
happenings and events that are in direct relation to the Word of God.

Prophecy is considered a divine inspiration, not a thought or
something thought of (divine—supremely good)! So a prophecy would
always be good and accomplish good.

It is written in Jeremiah 23:32, "Behold, I am against those who
prophesy lying dreams, says the Lord, and tell them and cause My

people to err and go astray by their lies and by their vain boasting and recklessness. Yet I did not send them or command them; nor do they profit these people at all, says the Lord." A common and special gift of prophecy would profit God's people, no profit = no prophet!

The real gift of prophecy is to be coveted by us, as written in 1 Corinthians 14:1: "Follow the way of love and eagerly desire spiritual gifts, especially the Gift of Prophecy." Down in verse 4 we see more definition: "He who speaks in a tongue edifies himself, but he who prophesies edifies the church." Edification is necessary in the church; we must exhort and edify one another, thus keeping ourselves built up on our most holy faith. Jude 1:20–23 says, "But you, dear friends, build yourselves up in your most holy faith and pray in the Holy Spirit. Keep yourselves in God's love as you wait for the mercy of our Lord Jesus Christ to bring you to eternal life. Be merciful to those who doubt; snatch others from the fire and save them; to others show mercy, mixed with fear—hating even the clothing stained by corrupted flesh."

Let us remember that "people are the opportunity"; we need to edify one another and reach out to help the unbelievers come into the saving knowledge of the Lord Jesus Christ, which is the good news about the kingdom. Amen! This good news was promised long ago by God through His prophets in the Holy Scriptures. We see this good news further in Paul's greeting to the Romans, in Romans 1:11: "For I long to visit you so I can share a spiritual blessing with you that will help you grow strong in the Lord. I am eager to encourage you in your faith, but I also want to be encouraged by yours. In this way, each of us will be a blessing to the other."

The Common Gift of Prophecy blesses the prophet and the people; we see this blessing when Saul sent men to capture David in 1 Samuel 19:19–24. In verse 19 we see that Saul is sending his troops to capture David, but when the troops arrived they saw Samuel and the other prophets prophesying. In verse 20 we read that the Spirit of

God came upon Saul's men, and they also began to prophesy. When Saul heard this he sent other troops, but when they arrived to capture David, they too began prophesying; when the Spirit of God comes on you, the outcome is catchy. Amen! The same thing happened a third time; then Saul himself went, and as we see down in verse 23, the Spirit of God came on Saul, and he began prophesying. It seems from these verses that we could say the Spirit of God is definitely in all prophecy.

What Saul had planned was interrupted and stopped by prophesy; a misdeed was turned into a testimonial service. The people of the town wondered at all this prophesying; they knew Samuel to be a prophet, but not all these! All can and should prophesy—that means you and me! As we read in Revelation 19:10, "For the testimony of Jesus is the Spirit of prophesy." Everybody can testify of Jesus and His goodness, thus everyone can and should prophesy.

Prophecy is inspired utterance in a known tongue. Inspired means: (a) to influence, move, or guide by divine or supernatural inspiration; (b) breathe or blow into or upon.

In John 20:22 we see, "And having said this, He breathed on them and said to them, receive the Holy Spirit." As we look in Acts 1:8 we see the power, ability, efficiency, and might come upon them when Jesus said, "The Holy Spirit will come upon you, and you will be my witnesses in the surrounding areas and all the world." A witness would testify of Jesus, thus prophesying of the good news about the kingdom of God. Amen!

Revelation is always part of prophesying. The Word of God allows us insight into the now. From biblical happenings, we get a fresh vision or direction from the Bible. When we speak this out as encouragement, it is common prophesy, inspired utterance in a known tongue.

The Holy Spirit is the Spirit of Truth, thus any leadings from Him would point directly to Jesus—the Light and the Truth. Amen!

Prophesying does not make one a prophet; the Bible says we would all prophesy; yes, this means you! In 1 Corinthians 14:5 we see, "Now I wish that you might all speak in tongues, but more especially (I want you) to prophesy (to be *inspired*, to preach and interpret the divine will and purpose). He who prophesies (who is *inspired* to preach and teach) is greater (more useful and more important) than he who speaks in tongues, unless he should interpret (what he says), so that the church may be edified and receive good (from it)."

To be inspired is to be outstanding or to have brilliance in a way suggestive of divine.

We have the Seed in each and every one of us to produce God kinds; Jesus was and is *That Seed!* Amen! Jesus gives us our spiritual freedom and has called us to it—freedom to prophesy, freedom to encourage, and freedom to love one another.

Our spiritual inspiration or prophesying causes unity, and unity totally destroys all of the devil's plans, which always causes division of some sort. Unity is like-mindedness, and spiritual unity causes a leading to share with one another, and sharing people have no lack; therefore, no division. Amen! The beginning church was positioned this way, and the Holy Spirit led everyone this way. Acts 2:43–47 says, "Then fear (the spirit of reverence), came upon every soul, and many wonders and signs were done through the Apostles (teachers). Now all who believed were together, and had all things in common (they had the Holy Spirit in common) and sold their possessions and goods, and divided them among all, as anyone had need (they were led to share)." Amen! "So continuing daily with *one accord* in the Temple, and breaking bread from house to house, they ate their food with gladness and simplicity of heart, praising God and having favor with all the people. And the Lord added daily those who were being saved."

This whole church, unity, and saving grace concept came out of prophecy. The prophecy of Joel, spoken by Peter to the men of Judea and all who dwell in Jerusalem, in Acts 2:14–21 says, "And it shall come to pass in the last days, says God. That I will pour out of My Spirit on all flesh; your sons and your daughters shall or will prophesy. Your young men shall (will) see visions; your old men shall (will) dream dreams. And on My menservants and on My maidservants I will pour out My Spirit in those days; and they shall (will) prophecy. I will show wonders in heaven above and signs in the earth beneath; blood and fire and vapors of smoke. The sun shall be turned into darkness, and the moon into blood, before the coming of the great and awesome day of the Lord. That whoever calls on the name of the Lord; shall be saved."

Wonders in heaven above and signs *in* the earth beneath! A wonder is a cause of astonishment, astonishment at something awesomely mysterious. God is going to show His glorious power to all in the heavenly realm. He will astonish everyone in heaven by revealing mysteries, mysteries kept from before any of us were, awesome abilities, awesome creations, awesome dwelling places, and all of our forerunners will receive the end of their faith. Amen! The perfecting of the saints in heaven and those of us on the earth at this culmination of the times will occur! We will be perfected together! Unity of the faith! Glory to God!

God also mentions signs *in* the earth beneath. A sign is something material or external that stands for or signifies something spiritual. *In* and not *on* the earth beneath; I believe God is not only revealing heaven as wonderful, but hell as real. Hell will be revealed as the spiritual dead, and the place of those whose spirits were and are dead. Spiritual will be revealed as real, saved; faith people will see the glorious revelation of heaven and God's glory shown in His Son Jesus! The devil is also very real and will be revealed as defeated, left with all who yielded to him in the smoking, vapor-filled, fire-engulfed hell.

So let us follow God's eternal wisdom; working according to His will and principles, let us judge all prophesies and utterances by the Bible. All godly prophesies will be in perfect harmony with the written Word of God and will cause light to go upon all situations, thus eliminating all doubt.

So let us covet earnestly these best gifts.

Yet!

Part 2: The Special Gift of Prophecy: Increased Awareness and Direction for and into the Future, through a Spoken Word, Received by Faith!

THE GREATEST PROPHECY EVER WAS the prophecy of Jesus, and how He would die for all. This one prophecy and its fulfillment has changed everyone's outcome, forever.

Fulfillment is a key word, as a true prophecy will be fulfilled, by God, and through people. The definition of fulfillment is to put into effect, to convert into reality. Fulfill is a verb, an action that produces the reality of a spoken word, divinely given. The prophecy about Jesus dying was given in John 11:51–52: "He did not say this on His own, but as high priest that year He prophesied that Jesus would die for the Jewish nation, and not only for that nation but also for the scattered children of God, to bring them together and make them one." In John chapter 19 this prophecy came to pass, which actually started with a prophecy by Isaiah. Read Isaiah chapter 53 to connect this great happening. Jesus was given for us. God's only and beloved Son, He paid the full price for us. Given as a ransom for us His people, we the believers have such a great High Priest! Amen!

Psalm 111: 7–9 says, "The works of His hands are faithful and just; all His precepts are trustworthy. They are established forever and ever, enacted in faithfulness and uprightness. He provided redemption for His people; He ordained His covenant forever—holy and awesome is His name." We have a guaranteed prophecy from David that became real and true in Jesus the man, and Jesus the Son of God. Oh, what a wonderful name!

Another noted phrase that was amplified above is (he was not self-moved). A prophecy is and should always be special and spontaneous. In 1 Corinthians 14:30–33 we read, "And if a revelation comes to someone who is sitting down, the first speaker should stop. For you can all prophesy in turn so that everyone may be instructed and encouraged. The spirits of prophets are subject to the control of prophets. For God is not a God of disorder but of peace—as in all the congregations of the Lord's people." We see in these scriptures many things: prophesies coming by inspiration (spontaneous); coming to more than one in the assembly but only one at a time; stimulation and encouragement; ability to control one's speech; and orderly, precise instruction causing peace to abound. As we stay connected to God through His Word, and have a desire and zeal to help people, He (God) will give us inspired utterance in a known tongue to lead ourselves as well as those around us.

On January 1, 2012, I received a gift of prophecy; I was actually seeking what the next step would be for my wife and I to do in the kingdom of God. As I was reading the Bible and pondering, almost elevating into the Spirit realm, this prophecy came to me: "Stay blameless and faithful, saith the Lord, and I will work in you freedom—freedom to teach, freedom to preach, freedom to touch, and freedom to love and be loved. I, the Lord, will do this; yea, I will do this unto you." Glory to God! This prophecy did exactly what a prophecy should do; it encouraged me, gave me hope, and also lined up with the Word of God. You see, many verses in the Bible talk about staying or remaining blameless, and we are actually commanded at times to be faithful. Amen! My wife and I both knew that this was our direction from God, given by the Holy Spirit through a gift of prophecy. It was just what we needed and was a ministering to us by the Spirit of God!

More than one in a gathering may have a divine revelation from God to minister to one another's needs; this is the order of God and is allowed and even cherished. Amen! Stimulation and encouragement are the heart of prophesy because the testimony of Jesus is the Spirit of all prophecy; it is love Himself caressing us with a word. A prophesy has a beginning and an end; the person or persons delivering these precious words know when the Holy Spirit is finished and should stop at this point. Orderly instruction causes peace to abound; let us follow that peace!

Philippians 4:6–7 says, "Do not be anxious about anything, but in every situation, by prayer and petition, with thanksgiving, present your requests to God. And the peace of God, which transcends all understanding, will guard your hearts and your minds in Christ Jesus."

I would like to key in on two words, human and spirit. We must be able to differentiate between the two to receive from God. Human is relating to the characteristics of humans, susceptible to the frailties of human nature. Spirit is the immaterial intelligence or sentient part of a person, the activating or essential principle influencing a person. Spiritual people have senses that are keen to God and His realm; a sentient person is sensitive to, and perceiving of, the supernatural.

A real prophecy is a supernatural word from God to encourage and propel His people to go further in their quest for Him and to advance the kingdom of God in the earth.

Let us covet earnestly these best gifts.

Yet!

CHAPTER 8

Common and Special Gifts of Tongues
A natural and supernatural utterance, inspired
by God, in an unknown tongue

**Part 1: The Common Gifts of Tongues and the
Interpretation Are Actually and Always Supernatural
in Essence; Therefore, These Gifts Would Always Be
Special in Nature—Our heightened prayer language
coupled with understanding from the Word of God.**

WE START BY LOOKING INTO the tongue as explained in Psalm 45:1:
"My heart is stirred by a noble theme as I recite my verses for the King;
my tongue is the pen of a skillful writer."

David used his tongue to speak forth revelation in regard to Jesus;
he spoke a lot in skillful songs and reflective poems, and love was the
theme of many of his tongues written. Amen!

The gift of tongues and the interpretation of tongues are given to
edify and encourage, and are as strong as prophecy for edifying the

church and setting forth direction. In Hebrews 2:1–4, we see hearing as an important part of any spoken word, by tongues of men or of angels. "We must pay the most careful attention, therefore, to what we have heard, so that we do not drift away. For since the message spoken through angels was binding, and every violation and disobedience received its just punishment, how shall we escape if we ignore so great a salvation? This salvation, which was first announced by the Lord, was confirmed to us by those who heard Him. God also testified to it by signs, wonders and various miracles, and by gifts of the Holy Spirit distributed according to His will."

The gifts of the Holy Spirit are controlled by the Holy Spirit—He giving power into the grace of God as He wills. This elevation of grace causes an effect in natural circumstances that enables supernatural events to flourish; tongues (prayer languages of the believer) are included in this heightened Holy Spiritual gifting. Praying with a Holy Spirit-given prayer language is necessary for spiritual development. The common speaking and praying in these types of tongues can and should reveal mysteries. Amen!

In 1 Corinthians 14:2, we see this verse as a foundation to praying out God's will and plan for us: "For anyone who speaks in a tongue does not speak to people but to God. Indeed, no one understands them; they utter mysteries by the Spirit."

Our praying and speaking in diverse tongues enables us communication into the God realm, a perception into the ways and purposes of God. Amazing! When we receive the Holy Spirit and the evidence of this infilling by a reception of our prayer language, this prayer language gives us entry into the spiritual realm, allowing us participation in and with all the other gifts of the Spirit, namely, the Word of Wisdom, the Word of Knowledge, Special Faith, Gifts of Healings, Miracles, and Prophesies. Our spirit in us is yearning and speaking out the mysteries of God, thus bringing supernatural or spiritual happenings into this earthly realm, attainable to all who believe.

There is a difference between the initial infilling and speaking versus the gift of tongues with interpretation. The first experience should be the believer receiving his or her greater prayer language, greater in depth and greater in ability. Amen! This prayer language is necessary to edify one's self and should be used daily to stay in tune with one's spirit and know the direction that the Holy Spirit is leading. "For those who are led by the Spirit of God are the children of God." This scripture is found in Romans 8:14 and is a foundation into all the Spirit has and is able to do in our lives.

Spirit-leading is learned and attained by staying in the Bible and praying in tongues. The experience of the baptism and reception of the Holy Spirit will have evidence associated with it, speaking with different and unknown tongues, unknown to the speaker, but known and received by God.

On the day of Pentecost many different languages were spoken, languages unknown to the speaker. In Acts 2:1–4 we see, "When the day of Pentecost came, they were all together in one place. Suddenly a sound like the blowing of a violent wind came from heaven and filled the whole house where they were sitting. They saw what seemed to be tongues of fire that separated and came to rest on each of them. All of them were filled with the Holy Spirit and began to speak in other tongues as the Spirit enabled them." Jesus had just told them of this infilling not many days before, in Acts 1:5. In Mark 16:17–18, Jesus also gave instruction about these tongues: "And these signs will accompany those who believe: In my name they will drive out demons; *they will speak in new tongues*; they will pick up snakes with their hands; and when they drink deadly poison, it will not hurt them at all; they will place their hands on sick people, and they will get well."

One (tongue of fire) sat on each of them, and this divine fire ignited their individual hearts and bound them to the Spirit of Jesus, who was left to comfort and guide us into all the *common and special* gifts of the Spirit. Amen! This divine fire or power accompanied their words and caused a penetration into the hearts of men. The miracle was not in the ears of the hearers but in the mouths of the speakers; this praising God with the tongues of the world was a precursor of what was to be expected as the good news penetrated the entire world, just as Jesus had commanded! Glory! This outpouring of the Spirit onto the apostles and shared with the people was indeed the means of rebuilding Jerusalem, in a spiritual sense, and was the foundation and state of the gospel church in the known world. So we can see that this reception of the Holy Spirit was received as a gift from God to replace the person of Jesus, His Paraclete.

The Holy Spirit, the third Person of the Trinity (Father, Son, and Holy Spirit), as Jesus had told them in John 14:15–17, "If you love me, keep my commands. And I will ask the Father, and He will give you another advocate to help you and be with you forever—the Spirit of truth. The world cannot accept Him, because it neither sees Him nor knows Him. But you know Him, for He lives with you and will be in you."

Our praying in tongues is supplied by the Spirit of Truth, a truth that stays with us and is in us forever; our prayer language is our God-given ability to make it all the way; the Spirit of Truth allows us to keep Jesus' commandments and show our love for Him.

This Spirit of Truth also allows us to see Him and know Him, a relationship the world or worldly folks will never experience. Let us always pray in tongues as the Holy Spirit gives us utterance, confirming and affirming our having and possessing the gift of tongues and furthering this gift by interpretation. Amen!

Let us covet earnestly these best gifts.

Yet!

Part 2: Special Tongues Are Given for a Specific Person, Group, or Season, Dividing Truth from Reason. Special Interpretation Is Truth Revealed through Human Vessels, God's Elect, for the Advancement of the Kingdom.

AS WE LOOK AT THE more advanced or specific tongues, let us not forget that praying in tongues is for all who have been baptized in the Holy Ghost. All are able and should speak with new tongues in edification of oneself, but not all will have the *gift* of a message in tongues.

Edifying and personal tongues, our prayer language, is for us to pray out the mysteries of God and God's will for us individually. We see this in Romans 8:26–27: "In the same way, the Spirit helps us in our weakness. We do not know what we ought to pray for, but the Spirit Himself intercedes for us through wordless groans. And He who searches our hearts knows the mind of the Spirit, because the Spirit intercedes for God's people in accordance with the will of God."

Psalm 139:1–4 says, "You have searched me, Lord, and You know me. You know when I sit and when I rise; You perceive my thoughts from afar, You discern my going out and my lying down; You are familiar with all my ways. Before a word is on my tongue, You, Lord, know it completely."

Let's define a few words in this passage. *Perceive is* to become aware of through the senses, especially seeing. More than just our eyes see things as real; our senses and our spiritual awareness perceive as real the things of God. When we see into the spirit, we perceive as real all the categories and concepts of God, Jesus, and the Holy Spirit; this seeing affords us a knowing, and this knowing becomes as real as anything we have physically seen with our eyes. By perception we receive faith as real; we receive hope from God as well. Romans 15:13

says, "May the God of hope fill you with all joy and peace as you trust in Him, so that you may overflow with hope by the power of the Holy Spirit." Hope is given by God, a gift, through the power of the Holy Spirit. This type of hope is a confident assurance that what you perceived in the Word of God will be seen in your natural, physical life. This is "a having" as real as what was "perceived" by your senses. Amen!

Of the three greatest of the realizations—faith, hope, and *love*— *love is the greatest* (1 Corinthians 13:13).

Love is our life; without it we will not exist. We must perceive God's love as real, a love that has no bounds, has no limits, and has no end. Thank you, God, for the love that was shed abroad in our hearts through the power of the Holy Spirit. Romans 8:38 says this love, Jesus' love, is bigger than death, bigger than life, bigger than angels, bigger than demons, bigger than fears, bigger than worries, and bigger than all the powers of hell, and it is all ours.

The second word I'd like to expound on is *discern*—to detect with senses other than vision and to come to know or recognize mentally. This word really sums up the perceiving we are talking about and solidifies our being able to receive as real all the categories and concepts of God, realizing the actual definition of understanding is the categories and concepts of God. The more we read the Bible and meditate on the things of God, the more our discernment increases, and the more power and ability we possess. Amen!

When we receive faith as real (faith: that inner witness connecting us to God's kingdom, and affording us the ability to bring and possess supernatural happenings from heaven and God's realm into our realm), faith is the substance of our lives! When we perceive hope as real (hope: confident trust with the expectation of fulfillment), and when love abides (love: the ultimate expression of God's loyalty, purity, and mercy extended toward His people), we are alive unto God, and His abilities become our abilities. Amen!

The last word to define is *tongue*—a fleshy, moveable, muscular process of the floors of the mouths of most vertebrates that bears sensory end glands, especially in taking and swallowing food and in humans as a speech organ. As a speech organ it has phonetic vocal folds or cords, thus allowing sound formation and speech. So to apply tongues to our text, *special tongues* and interpretation, we see that our tongue or our dialect is actually a learned inner communication with like beings, spirits, or subjects. It is so! It is our communication with God in the spirit realm, and then our ability to possess this outcome in the earth, and gives us the ability to interact with one another. Wow! We find these special tongues at work in Isaiah 50:4: "The Sovereign Lord has given me a well-instructed tongue, to know the word that sustains the weary. He wakens me morning by morning, wakens my ear to listen like one being instructed." This verse exemplifies our definition of what a special gift of tongues is for, "the edification of a certain individual or group, making aware the kingdom of God."

As I was driving down the interstate one day, listening to my favorite godly teachings, I felt impressed to pray in tongues. As I was praying, a word kept coming out—"Costa, Costa"—so I wrote this word down and knew this was the answer to a question I had been asking God: Where do my wife and I fit in the body of Christ? What should we be doing for God and His people? As I returned home from work that day, I knew I needed to find the definition or, more importantly, the interpretation of this word, *Costa*. I knew it was the answer to my question. As I found this word in the Greek translation of the Bible, it meant "rib," I was very excited that God had created my wife and I to be "ribs." You see, the definition of a rib is taken from one body to form another, as with Adam and Eve, and a protector of the vital organs of the body; I was thrilled because I know God uses the natural to help us understand the spiritual. I had an understanding where I fit, and what a great peace there is in finding your place in Him. Amen!

Our receiving of the Holy Spirit and our evidence of this infilling is speaking with different kinds of tongues. These tongues, as with all the categories and concepts of God, should grow as we grow in Him, feeding our spirit on His Word, developing a likeness to Him. Amen!

We are truly created in His image and likeness, and as we grow strong in the Spirit we realize a common bond to the King of Kings, the Spirit He left us to show us things to come.

The Holy Spirit is given to take the place of Jesus Christ, thus affording us an ability to make His will known by praying out mysteries and future events, separating truth from reason. This interpretation of tongues comes to us by simply being able to translate into a known tongue what has been spoken in an unknown language. It is a simple yet complex gift of the Holy Spirit given as He wills and to whom He wills.

We are actually in the Spirit realm when we receive these spiritual abilities, utterances, and explanations of God's plan for our lives and those he has joined us to.

Tongues and their interpretation, as with all the gifts of the Holy Spirit, will be done with order and in line with the Word of God, *always*.

As we grow in our freedoms that God has given us, let us realize the need of the people around us; let us operate in the grace of God, always willing to assist, always approving what is just and true, and always being in the likeness and image of Jesus Christ, our Savior, Friend, and Redeemer.

I will covet earnestly all these best gifts of the Holy Spirit.

Yet!

God says, "I will show you a more excellent way, Love."

God is love!

PRAYER FOR SALVATION AND BAPTISM OF THE HOLY SPIRIT

Heavenly Father, I come to You in the Name of Jesus. Your Word says, "And everyone who calls on the name of the Lord will be saved" (Acts 2:21). I am calling on You. I pray and ask Jesus to come into my heart and be Lord over my life according to Romans 10:9–10: "If you declare with your mouth, 'Jesus is Lord,' and believe in your heart that God raised him from the dead, you will be saved. For it is with your heart that you believe and are justified, and it is with your mouth that you profess your faith and are saved." I do that now. I confess that Jesus is Lord, and I believe in my heart that God raised Him from the dead.

I am now reborn! I am a Christian—a child of Almighty God! I am saved! You also said in Your Word, "If you then, though you are evil, know how to give good gifts to your children, how much more will your Father in heaven give the Holy Spirit to those who ask him!" (Luke 11:13). I'm also asking You to fill me with the Holy

Spirit. Holy Spirit, rise up within me as I praise God. I fully expect to speak with other tongues as You enable me (Acts 2:4). In Jesus' name. Amen!

Begin to praise God for saving you and filling you with the Holy Spirit. Speak those words and syllables you receive—not in your own language, but the language given to you by the Holy Spirit. You have to use your own voice. God will not force you to speak. Don't be concerned with how it sounds; it is a heavenly language! Continue praising God and praying in this new language every day.

You are a born-again, Spirit-filled believer! You will never be the same!

Find a good, Spirit-filled church that boldly preaches the Word of God and obeys it. Become part of a church family who will love and care for you as you love and care for them. We need to be connected to each other. It increases our faith and strengthens us in our walk with God. It is God's plan for us.

God bless you in your new life in Him as you walk out the gifts of His Spirit, amen!

Acts 2:21; Romans 10:9; John 3:5-6, 15-16; Romans 8:9-11; Luke 11:13; Acts 2:4

ACKNOWLEDGMENTS

This book came into creation by and because of the tireless faith of my pastor and his wife. I spent thousands of hours listening to his many God-given teaching series. All of my pastor's teachings are made available free of charge, so, as he says, no charge means no excuses. Amen! Let us covet earnestly our pastors and teachers, and truly thank God for the feet upon which they're sent.

ABOUT THE AUTHOR

Jerry was raised in the Midwest with a simple, modest lifestyle, seemingly happy with the normal procession of life, school, career, marriage, child, and dog. But after trying many substitutes to fill the void in his life, he proceeded with his wife's prompting to go on a quest after the Holy Spirit. It was a spiritual journey starting right around the new millennium, not because a century was beginning but because Jerry's new-found life was beginning—a spiritual life that has a beginning but knows no end, the victory over every challenge that had been present in his life and those to come. It is a freedom that catapulted him into every form of happiness he experiences today: a oneness with God, his wife, and one another. Carry on!